INTRODUCTION

In the present volume Professor Hollingworth makes a distinctive and notable contribution to applied psychology. The problem is an ancient one: that of determining the qualities of men with reference to their fitness for the work of the world. The general problem precedes the special one alike in theory and in practice. The earliest solutions were in the nature of ambitious attempts to read the ear-marks of mental ability in outward signs; under the incentive of the growth of science these gave way to such systems as phrenology and physiognomy. Such revelations, decisive if sound, proved to be vain hopes or hopelessly irrelevant. The impressionistic verdicts gained from actual experience reflected the cumulative acumen of discernment which ever was and remains the issue of wisdom, empirical but authentic. It furnishes suggestive clues to investigation and a check upon its results. The problem came to its own when the modern science of psychology gave it its setting in the rapid accumulation of knowledge and technique for the interpretation of mental qualities. It at once established the futility of ambitious leads and the necessity of careful, patient and discerning analysis. The present volume surveys the field of attained results and the method of their attainment, in this engaging research.

Central in interest and promise stands the psychological test. In so far as psychology has laid bare the fundamental qualities upon which achievement depends, its application has developed a series of tests to determine how the individual compares with the others or with the average in respect to this, that, and the other constituent quality. Professor Hollingworth presents the results of such analysis, both in relation to the variety of human traits and in the grading of individuals by reference to the measure of the quality which each possesses. The enumeration is at best provisional, but in its totality cannot go far wrong in establishing the measure of a man. It includes the qualities which can hardly be determined otherwise than by an impressionistic judgment, as well as those appraised by actual achievement under test. There results a mental scale of general ability, adequate to gauge normality and to suggest practical standards of superiority or deficiency.

The question at once arises: how far are the qualities desirable for this or that vocation of a general order, and how far are they specific in their demands. In this respect vocations differ widely. The musical vocation exemplifies a specialized profession depending upon a proficiency that is largely a dower of heredity; yet within this field the psychological test has proved its efficiency by determining the still more specialized facilities that jointly compose the psychology of the musician. In further pursuit of insight the psychological laboratory has undertaken to analyze the qualities needed for the several specialties of modern vocational life, by setting up "test" counterparts of practical occupations, by reducing them to their underlying facilities, by testing the correlation of quality and achievement, and by combining the clues or verdicts of several methods. Conclusions depend for their value upon logical caution and the technical methods which have been developed to meet these applications. All this is as yet but a program or a limited beginning in its execution; but it is a program well founded in principle and already in part available in practice.

A group of collateral interests supports the enterprise and yields valuable results. The interest in unusual men has led to the psychograph or psychological analysis of the qualities of great men, as an individual study. Men fall into types, by temperament and achievement, by heredity and career. The type makes definite the larger contours of human differences and reveals their specific combination; the charm of biography is psychological as well as historical. The vital import of heredity—practically expressed in the eugenic movement—finds recognition in the study of correlation of traits in those near of kin. Evolution leads to prediction; early taste, talent, achievement, precocity foreshadow ultimate capacity; we learn how far the child is father to the man, how far we may see the future in the early expressions and with what limitations the environment molds character. The most valued because most authentic type of biography is autobiography. Self-analysis is intimate if unreliable, but by this token worthy of study. Professor Hollingworth's contribution to the measure of reliance to be placed upon one's judgment of self in comparison with one's judgment of others and others' judgment of him forms an interesting original study—one of many—incorporated in these chapters.

Of distinctive status are the tests of ability presented by life itself and by the conventional institutions which compose the social environment. The processes of education, the rate of advance, the comparative readiness with which one or another discipline is absorbed and mastered: these are at once preparations for life and accredited tests of ability. For these reasons such "school" qualities are subjected to a special study; and fairly conclusive results indicate to what measure they must be supplemented, if not superseded, by the designed psychological test, to meet the conditions of actual selection and employment of men. At this point the several methods converge; for the vocations have a vital interest in the school, as has the school in vocational application of its discipline and training. The actual comparison of results, especially by the method of correlation, has already established the degree of relation—and eventually of coöperation—to be expected of the two. In all these ways has painstaking method supplemented and replaced impressionism, haphazard opinion been supported or overturned by accumulation of fact, and the scientific approach to the study of vocational fitness become firmly established. The road from theory to practice, if it is to be well built and enduring, must be laid on careful foundation. To such an end this volume is a worthy contribution.

No question of vocational fitness has been more eagerly discussed than the contrasted fitness of men and women, and the consequent basis of differentiation of career desirable or necessary for the two, both as wage-earners and in every other relation of life. A discussion of this problem from the point of view of this volume is wisely included, and in turn a definite negative conclusion reached. It is shown that in the main capacities tested—with several and significant exceptions—men and women, boys and girls, are comparable; individual differences outweigh sex differences. The interpretation of this result will not be uniform, even when due allowance is made for the range of tests responsible for the conclusion. The biologist will continue to insist upon the significance of fundamental differences; the experiences of life reinforce as they express the fact that men and women live with as well as upon a different perspective of psychological equipment; the psychologist may suggest that the tests and comparisons—based in large measure upon comparable and derivative facilities—naturally bring forth the parallel measure in which secondary qualities yield similar issues. It must be noted how largely a large share of conventional vocations call upon specialized and late varieties of intellectual traits; for these precisely, men and women may have comparable fitness, while none the less psychologically contrasted in realms closer to natural function. Women have proved that they are as fit to study—and, if you like, to vote—as are men; as fit to enter and succeed in vocations in terms of tested qualifications. How far the less measurable and collateral qualities make them fit and successful on a different basis, and still leave them contrasted in fundamental reactions, is a very different question. It is well to understand the bearing as well as the range of the ascertained facts of the case.

The modern man and the modern woman live upon the upper ranges of their qualities, and in no respect more momentously than in respect to those qualities exercised and demanded by vocational fitness. In the biological sense they are all highly specialized, refined, derivative, secondary issues of qualities that had a limited scope in the primitive form of life in which the race achieved its maturity and established its psychology. The problem of civilization is to train these original traits of man to the specific cherished purposes of the work of the world. The life of the mind is as highly artificial as the life of the cities; for such is the condition of the twentieth century. Yet the primitive man survives and asserts his own; life is not all vocation. Social and industrial complexity dominates the expressions of human psychology. To unite a comprehension of their foundations with skill in applying their demands is the business of the "applied" psychologist. The present contribution, it is hoped, will prove a helpful aid to those who are striving to understand as well as to those who must apply with what wisdom they command, the available resources of human nature.

JOSEPH JASTROW.

CHAPTER I

MOTIVES AND ANTECEDENTS OF VOCATIONAL PSYCHOLOGY

VOCATIONAL EFFORTS OF PRIMITIVE MAGIC

Among very primitive people we find the recognition already established that the course of the individual's fortune depends on two distinct factors: external forces and personal characteristics. Individuals similar in type experience different fortunes because of the different external events that attend their respective careers. Equally, individuals of however diverse characteristics suffer the same fortunes at the hands of some common or identical external occurrence. Two combatants of equal skill and valor are rendered unequal by a defective lance; two runners equally swift are made unequal by a pebble in the path; a vigorous babe fails to mature properly because of pestilence, war, or famine. On the other hand, both old and young, weak and strong, stupid and cunning, are alike reduced to helplessness in the face of flood, earthquake, and forest fire.

Primitive thinking, in its attempts to control the course of personal fortune, thus had its attention directed to two groups of factors, each of which it sought to control by such means as it could at the moment devise. A very early stage of such thinking took the form of the belief that *desire* could impress itself on the course of physical events and also on the development of personal characteristics. The expression of desire, either of the individual immediately concerned or of others more remotely involved, was consequently invoked and declared in more or less emphatic and overt form as a determining factor in personal fortune. In many cases this expression was given some indirect or symbolic form, as in gesture, ritual, tableau, masquerade, and imitative portrayal.

On the side of physical factors this attempt took the form of crude magic, adjuration, sacrifice, and incantation, all of which were calculated to dispose the physical elements favorably toward the individual concerned in the ceremonials. Crude ritual observances and ceremonies, such as sacrifice, mimicry, and tableau, were believed to influence in some occult way the growth of crops, the changes in weather, the health of enemies, the movements of game, the supply of fish, etc. A typical fishing expedition among the natives of the Caroline Islands aptly illustrates this point of view. The chief official is not an expert boatman nor a fisher, but the medicine man of the tribe. He owes his authority not to his knowledge of the habits and haunts of fish, but to his store of incantations and exorcisms. Various rites are conducted before embarking. The fishermen must leave the island without speaking; and especially, the purpose of the expedition must not be mentioned aloud. A "luck" formula is pronounced over the boat. Sacrifices of special foods are offered, lest the lines be broken by sharks or tangled in the rocks. In Mexico, an elaborate pantomime, representing the harvesting of crops, was staged annually at a religious festival. This was believed sufficient to produce the good crops which were desired for the next season. Special dances were performed by persons representing the various vegetables which were particularly coveted.

Among primitive races in almost every part of the world one finds magical properties attributed to a sort of toy which anthropologists call the "bull roarer." It consists merely of a flat stick, attached to the end of a cord. When whirled around it produces a roaring or humming sound which easily reminds one of the rumble of wind, the roll of thunder, or the distant cry of an animal. In various quarters this instrument is used in a ceremonial way. Since its sound resembles thunder, it is used as a charm against that form of physical violence. Because of its resemblance to both thunder and wind, it is incorporated in elaborate rain-making mysteries. Sometimes it is used to drive or call wild or domesticated animals, and hence comes to be used as a means of bringing luck to hunters. Figures and emblems, carved on the slab of wood, are supposed to specify the particular kind of luck or fortune which the individual seeks.

On the side of personal characteristics the same endeavor took the form of blessings, incantations, dedications, curses, prayers and petitions, the wearing of symbolic charms and the submission of the infant or youth to a variety of prenatal and childhood experiences and ceremonials. Thus it is believed that by appropriating a dead man's spear and thereby expressing a desire for his skill and valor, these traits of character will pass to the new owner. Boys are tossed into the air to make them grow tall, and rubbed with crystals and snake-skins to make them clever and intrepid medicine men. By scratching lifelike sketches of bison, deer, and fish on rocks, walls, and weapons, the savage hunter sought to acquire otherwise unattainable adroitness and success. "Disease or death may be produced by operating on the cuttings of a person's hair, the parings of his nails, or the remains of his food, when the person himself is far away. By wearing tiger's teeth a man may make himself brave and fierce." By drinking the blood of bulls he may become stalwart and powerful. The Ojibway Indian, in order to hurt his enemy and thus further his own interests, makes a small image of him and pierces it with a needle in the faith that the enemy will suffer. In order to terminate the latter's career he burns or buries the effigy, uttering magic words as he does so.

Remnants of this primitive magic still persist in the "psychological underworld," and many an old-wives' practice and incantation is in various quarters still believed or professed to further the course of the individual's fortune, or to jeopardize it, by rendering natural forces more benign or malignant, or by exerting some occult molding influence on the infantile abilities and propensities. Thus it is not at all uncommon, even in these days, for children to be dedicated at birth to the ministry, the missionary field, the service of the king, or to some particular cause or propaganda. A woman of the writer's acquaintance, solicitous for the future welfare of her babe, read solid and serious books during gestation in order to balance the emotional influences due to her absorption in music teaching during that period. Many practices of the most superstitious kind are resorted to in order to predetermine the sex, and hence the vocational prospects, of children yet unborn. Reliance on prayer as an effective agent in changing the course of events or the disposition and habits of some other individual is by no means confined to savages. Petitions that a neighbor may lose his appetite for drink, recover his lost eyesight, or find his wallet are as current in modern times as are official days of prayer for rain. Seeking to influence public opinion by the passing of formal resolutions, and modifying character, curing diseases and prolonging life through "absent treatment," the laying on of hands, the contemplation of relics, visitation of shrines, and concerted supplication, are practices which find high warrant in contemporary life. The essential idea behind all these practices seems to be the simple faith that nothing will interfere with the realization of desire, if only that desire is indicated by a method which has official or traditional sanction. The true nature of cause and effect and the conception of natural law are not yet realized on this level of thought.

THE PRACTICES OF MEDIEVAL CLAIRVOYANCE

A more advanced stage in the development of such thinking is indicated by the recognition that both the series of physical events and the individual endowment follow laws which transcend the personal desires of men. Nature comes to be recognized as a system of facts and connections. Both control and foresight henceforth seek to base themselves on the utilization of these stable laws and relationships. Instead of willing the individual's fortune to be thus and so, there is an earnest endeavor to seek for signs and clues of what that fortune is inevitably destined to be. Fortune-making becomes fortune-telling. The accidents and accompaniments of birth, the momentary positions of the planets, the calendar incidents, the hour or day of birth, the local meteorological conditions, birth-marks, stigmata, physiognomic and anthropometric characteristics, the folds of the flesh, the lines of the hand, the mode of birth: every fact that can participate in a relation of coincidence with the birth of the individual is selected as a sign of some future state of affairs, desirable or untoward, in the fortune of the individual, of his personal, domestic and occupational career.

Thus, in a recently published guide to character analysis based on ancient astrological pretensions, the following characteristics are asserted to belong to those who are born in the month of February:

"Those born in this month are very intuitive and good judges of character and human nature. They are successes in mercantile interests and enterprises. It is said that the best wives are born in this month, being always faithful and devoted. Great sincerity and power are possible for those born in this month. They rise to great heights and on the other hand are inclined to sink to the lowest depths. At times they are inclined to be melancholy, a tendency which they may overcome.

"Most February persons have good taste, are quick at absorbing information, and intuitive. One of their great faults is that they are inclined to be intolerant and cannot make themselves think from another's point of view.

"Their most common diseases are of the nervous and rheumatic orders. They should guard their actions on the ninth and sixteenth day of each month. Luck day, Saturday. Favorite colors, all shades of blue, pink, and Nile green. Lucky stones, sapphire, opal, or turquoise. Lucky numbers, 5 and 7. They will excel in music and art, and should marry with those born in October, January, or June."

Hardly less common than faith in the horoscope is belief in the detailed prophecies of palmistry. The following is a direct reproduction of paragraphs from a well-known metropolitan American newspaper, of the year 1915 (A. D.), headed, "What Your Fingers Mean:"

"Shorter palm and longer fingers, these show an aptitude for doing small things well. Their owners analyze everything, are supersensitive over trifles, often feeling unintentional slights. When these fingers are slim, as well as longer than the palm, they give to one the quality of diplomacy. Card sharps and gamblers have these long, slim, smooth fingers. The average-length fingers with an ordinary-sized palm show a well-balanced mind, with a thoroughly commonplace nature. When long fingers (with shorter palm) are knotted at the joints we find an extreme love for the minor parts of construction, whether it be in the building of a bridge or the endless tasks pertaining to a kitchen."

The same thing happens in the case of the individual's own acts. Every petty move and caper is taken to be significant of his future disposition, powers, or achievements. The first word the child utters, the first object for which he reaches, the animal he first imitates, the form of his earliest play activities, nothing that can be identified and described but comes to possess, in someone's mind, some peculiar significance and prognostic value. "Homely in the cradle, lovely at the table," is an oft-quoted maxim among hopeful mothers. "Happy is the bride that the sun shines on," has doubtless served to postpone more than one nuptial ceremony, and being "born under an unlucky star" has equally often afforded a certain consolation for personal awkwardness. A father of the writer's acquaintance believed his boy destined to follow the career of a druggist or pharmacologist, because, as a child, "he was so fond of playing with bottles and of pouring water from one into the other." Any lack of submissive devotion to a rubber doll is calculated to fill the parent's heart with apprehension and dire forebodings for the domestic peace of his daughter. War-babies and infants born on the high seas are envied for their romantic prospects. Illegitimate children are expected to be idiotic or else to be especially gifted with some poetic form of talent.

Belief in vocational magic and clairvoyance is clearly not entirely confined to medieval days. Nor is it true that such instances as those just cited arise only as material for frivolous conversations or as journalistic space-fillers in a dearth of more serious copy. So firmly are these superstitions established among large classes of people that special legislation is required to prevent their exploitation at the hands of crafty fakers. The fortune-teller is far from being a romantic and vestigial institution; and the type of prophecy which medieval clairvoyance represents continues to provide many with a substitute for more rigorous and less exciting inquiry.

MODERN PERIOD OF GUIDANCE AND SELECTION

However, as knowledge develops, a third stage is reached, in which we may be said to be moving, even though somewhat slowly, in our own scientific and educational work. This stage is marked by relative inattention to the series of physical events and by special emphasis on the original nature of the individual and on changes wrought in that original nature through the experiences of school life and other forms of educational process. The conditions and environmental factors of life have become so plastic that individuals can fairly easily find congenial environment and occupational material near at home or far from it, if only they know for what environment and material their natural powers are best adapted. Modern life, whether in city or in country, has become so diversified and labor so divided, that a small community affords the vocational variety which only a few years ago was quite unfamiliar to it. Moreover, the various avenues of communication, transportation and coöperation have become so elaborate that workers in one part of a nation can with little difficulty profit by activities and opportunities existing in distant places. Each branch of industry, commerce and art, as well as each professional and occupational activity, provides not only for a larger number of workers but for a greater variety as well. There is thus a tendency for the individual at an early point in his career, not only to adapt himself to an environment already provided, but to a certain degree to select that environment for which his abilities and interests seem best to fit him.

Attempts at controlling fortune, as now exercised, are neither magical nor clairvoyant. They take the rational, selective form of fitting the individual to the place for which his natural aptitudes best adapt him, so far as these facts of adaptability are discoverable, and so far as the environment is plastic or optional. This is at least the description of the process in democratic conditions of society. In countries in which hereditary aristocracy and caste systems still exist, the fortune of the individual is determined to a considerable extent by his birthright, by the occupation of his father, above all by sex—all dominated by tradition. Within this field of guidance and selection, activity has developed rather independently in two different directions. There has been on the one hand the notion that all the individual needs for a satisfactory occupational adjustment is knowledge of available opportunities, and appropriate technical training for the occupation of his choice. This point of view is seen in our own country in the popularizing of general education.

Under this conception general education, instead of being the prerogative of the ruling or moneyed class, is urged as a common right, a social duty and an economic necessity. Learning is not limited to those who expect to enter the theological, medical, legal, or academic professions. A certain amount of elementary school-knowledge, or at least of school-attendance, comes to be required of every prospective worker. Even the feeble-minded are labored with in the attempt to bring them up to their highest possible academic level. Boys and girls alike are not only urged but compelled to equip themselves with the knowledge of the elementary formal subjects; and the community taxes itself to furnish the teachers, the books, and the necessary physical paraphernalia. In this earlier form of educational theory little effort is made to give immediate applicability to the subject-matter of the curriculum. Classical studies with very little relevance to contemporary life; dead languages, with only a feeble claim to concrete serviceability;

formal exercises in designing and constructing useless bric-a-brac; trivial geographical, astronomical, anatomical, and military details: these are the subject-matter of the "general education." Back of their selection lies of course the doubtful conception that the general powers or faculties of the student are thereby cultivated, and that these may then be brought to bear effectively on any vocational activity which may be chosen.

The subject-matter is selected, not because of its interest or its utility, but mainly because of its difficulty and its formal character. Parental compulsion, vague social tendencies and impulses, petty personal rivalries, fondness for the teacher, and general cultural aspiration are relied on to facilitate the work of administration and to provide incentive. The "life-career" motive is but little utilized, and tends on the whole to be discouraged as sordid and commercial. But it is nevertheless believed that the grammatical, geographical, historical, and arithmetical elements will in the long run enable the pupil not only to enjoy life but to find it as well, or at least to be of the greatest possible service in the work into which he or she drifts. Only in the case of those who are utterly incompetent to deal with the general subject-matter, the feeble-minded, the blind, and the deaf, is this formal education willingly abandoned in favor of some definitely serviceable "industrial" training.

THE METHODS OF INDUSTRIAL EDUCATION

Quickly following this effort of the public schools to guide every boy and a few girls into successful careers through general education, came the realization that literary, linguistic, and mathematical information alone is inadequate to this task. It was felt by many that industrial or vocational education, calculated to fit the individual directly for his or her life occupation, should be begun at a much earlier age than that at which the group choosing the professions entered upon their further studies in the higher technical schools. It became obvious that many pupils terminated their public-school education as soon as they had satisfied the minimal requirements of the compulsory education law. These engaged at the earliest possible opportunity in some immediately gainful occupation. The occupations into which they commonly drifted were such as called for only a slight amount of intelligence and promised proportionately little by way of further equipment or promotion. They have come to be called "blind alley" occupations, and refer to such work as that of errand boys, elevator and telephone operators, small clerks, domestic servants, nursemaids, messengers, delivery boys, and teamsters.

Meanwhile those who had continued in school and completed the high-school curriculum emerged without special vocational fitness, and even without any knowledge of the vocational possibilities of their age and locality. The further development of vocational and industrial education of special sorts was then supplemented by general instruction in the vocational opportunities available. Vocational surveys were initiated for the purpose of acquiring information which could be placed in the hands of pupils and of those in charge of their training. These surveys made systematic inquiry into the vocational opportunities afforded to young people by the industries and enterprises of the vicinity. The assistance of employers was sought in the effort to learn the requirements of the various types of work; the nature of the labor involved; the wages; the general conditions, such as healthfulness, danger, companionship, and instruction; the rate of promotion; the prospect of future advancement. Such information has in many cases been published in pamphlets and bulletins and thus made accessible to teachers, pupils, and parents.

Along with this tendency went the attempt to give the pupil some first-hand knowledge of and immediate experience with the materials, implements, and products of the various industries from among which he or she might be expected to choose after leaving the school. This has been a difficult step to bring about, partly because of the various technical and administrative difficulties which it involved. Occasional hasty visits to mills, factories, stores, shops, offices, laboratories, and similar busy places give the pupil but a superficial notion of the actual work of the operations there observed. More extended and intensive observation, on the other hand, with perhaps an actual trial at the work, means a corresponding limitation of the range of institutions inspected. Talks by managers and foremen are likely to give only a dramatized view of the facts. School industries, on the other hand, cannot easily be organized and conducted in a manner technically complete and industrially representative. The result has been a growing tendency to push the vocational training further and further back into the earlier years of the curriculum, thus displacing much of the purely formal subject-matter.

With this change have come various experiments in study-practice methods, in which part of the day or term is spent at the general academic work, and part in actual service in a tentatively chosen form of industrial or commercial activity.

In this movement but little recognition was given to the psychological differences and peculiarities of the individuals concerned. Knowledge of personal aptitudes and capacities, interests, and satisfactions, was more or less taken for granted in each case, or at least left to develop in its own way. It was assumed either that any individual could satisfactorily pursue any vocation in which he might become interested, or else that industrial and vocational information alone was needed in order to enable the individual to make a suitable choice. Nor was there any doubt that the work which the youth found interesting and attractive at the time was the work in which he might find a maximum of ultimate success, satisfaction, and serviceableness. With the vocational surveys, the industrial schools, and the part-time practice methods of education we shall not be concerned, in what is to follow. They represent a movement of tremendous social and educational significance, but their development does not immediately concern that other field of work which we have designated "vocational psychology." They proceed mainly by giving the individual a knowledge of the external series of facts and events, thus replacing the era of fortune-telling and clairvoyance, with its search for signs and omens, just as fortune-telling had, in its own day, replaced the practices of crude objective magic. But the methods of industrial and occupational training have been found to solve only one aspect of the vocational problem; and it is more and more coming to be realized that a thorough understanding of the aptitudes which the individual brings to his work is as important as the knowledge of the opportunities which the environment affords. In the remainder of this book we shall be concerned with the various systematic efforts that have been made or are now being made to study the individual himself, and to judge from a determination of his mental characteristics the type of vocational activity which he is best fitted to undertake with success.

CHAPTER II

THE SEARCH FOR PHRENOLOGICAL AND PHYSIOGNOMIC PRINCIPLES

THE RISE OF EXPERIMENTAL SCIENCE

The primitive magic, directed toward the formation of individual character, was displaced by the personal clairvoyance which attempted to diagnose the individual's mental and moral constitution on the basis of his own early acts, expressions, and physical characteristics. This soon gave way to a tendency to abandon, for the most part, such signs as did not relate in some actual or fancied way, to the individual's brain. This limitation of the field of significant signs may be related to the widespread interest in human physiology, historically associated with the knowledge of anatomy. The invention of the microscope, Harvey's proof of the circulation of the blood, the discussion centering about the automaton theory of Descartes, and the rapid development of surgical technique, brought about a most interesting spread of curiosity concerning the nature and mechanism of the human body. Balls and tournaments gave way to dissections and demonstrations as means of courtly entertainment. Celebrated surgeons exhibited their skill and knowledge, and lectured on the facts of physiology and anatomy in the formal presence of royalty and society. Court painters executed pictures such as "The Anatomy Lesson," some of them now cherished as famous masterpieces.

Especially keen became the interest in the skull and brain in which, as Descartes taught, might be found the seat of the soul. Among the earliest of the rough discoveries was that concerned with the localization of special sensory and motor functions of the organism in particular regions of the brain. It was observed that irritation of certain parts of the surface or "cortex" of the brain, in cases where a portion of the skull had been removed, was followed by movement of particular parts of the body, and that individuals who had suffered from injury to certain parts of the brain seemed, on recovery, to be quite their usual selves, except that certain special capacities, as for instance the function of speech, were interfered with or quite destroyed. The unitary soul, described by Descartes as probably having its seat in the pineal gland, now bade fair to disintegrate into various minor faculties, each with its separate brain mechanism and its particular abode in some region of the skull.

The discovery of these elementary facts of brain localization was at once hit upon with zeal by those most interested in the means of foresight into human fortunes. Ignoring the fact that the localized features were simply the control of other parts of the body, as eyes, ears, limbs, speech organs, and the like, these enthusiasts leaped to the conclusion that every trait of character and every mental aptitude, every virtue and vice, ability, interest and capacity, had each its own shelf or pew in the brain area. Moreover, it was taken for granted that the relative development of these various characteristics was indicated by the depressions, projections and proportions of the skull bones. Here was light indeed on the destinies of men, their fitnesses and propensities, their appropriate choice of work and play! The enthusiasm and ardor that went into the elaboration of the new clairvoyance of phrenology would have meant most valuable increase in our knowledge of brain physiology had it been directed exclusively toward further legitimate inquiry. But the urgent desire for control and foresight was too great for practice to keep the slow pace of scientific fact.

Hastily the prophets drew up complicated and minute maps of the surface of the cranium and assigned to each recognizable patch some "faculty" which stood for an important mental or moral trait. Casual examination of the skulls of friends who chanced to possess particularly marked traits to an extreme degree was in some cases relied on to give guidance in the assignment of these patches to the respective traits. In some of the schemes the human traits conceived were so numerous that the bilateral symmetry and functions of the brain were ignored, and the two sides of the skull were assigned quite different functions. Thus arose phrenology, one of the most persistent fallacies of vocational analysis. This movement was founded by Gall and Spurzheim, two physicians and anatomists, in the latter part of the eighteenth century.[1] With the customary naïveté of the medical science of their time, they overestimated the significance of casual observations and fragmentary discoveries, and thus gave impetus to the exaggerated and extravagant claims made by their enthusiastic followers. "Phrenological societies" developed so rapidly and so widely that the movement became relatively independent of the scientific investigations which should have served to qualify and criticize its doctrines. Its propaganda were so vigorous and the practical needs which it promised to satisfy were so insistent, that even today many people hold tenaciously to its dicta. Scores of professionals thrive on their lucrative practice of its dogmas, and university graduates smile in a guilty way when asked, "Do you believe in phrenology?"

The tenacious persistence of phrenology, the degree to which it is resorted to and paid for by inquiring and earnest seekers after satisfactory paths through life, make it seem worth while to present a brief statement of the numerous errors and flagrant stupidities on which the practice of phrenology is based. It may also be worth while to suggest some of the rather interesting subsidiary reasons for its persistence as a cherished popular delusion and even as a topic for current scientific discussions and papers.

THE ASSUMPTIONS AND ERRORS OF PHRENOLOGY

Underlying all of the various phrenological systems were four common assumptions which briefly stated, were:

1. That such cerebral localization as exists is of fundamental and specific traits of character or types of ability, such as secretiveness, circumspection, love of babies, generosity, veneration, constructiveness, etc.

2. That the more developed any one of these given traits is, the larger will be the supposed area of the brain which contains its supposed organ.

3. That, since the skull fits fairly closely to the brain surface, the relative development of a given portion of the brain will be indicated by the relative prominence or size of the different parts of the cranium, so that the degree of possession of the trait may be judged from an examination of the exterior of the skull.

4. That the occasional casual observation of coincidence between particularly marked mental qualities and particular cranial characteristics is a sufficient basis for inferring universal and necessary connection between these two features.

Each of these assumptions involves obvious error and misapprehension in the light of what is now known concerning the nature of the human mind and the structure and functions of the brain. In order that these fallacies may be clearly disclosed the four main assumptions will be examined independently in the order in which we have here presented them.

1. In the first place, the only sort of localization of functions that has been authentically established is the projection, upon the brain structure, of the other parts of the organism, and the localization of sensory-motor centers which function in the connection of these various organs. Thus it is known that each of the principal groups of muscles of the body has its so-called center in the brain. From this part of the brain to the muscles concerned run bundles of motor-nerve fibers, so that activity in that particular part of the brain may result in the conduction of nervous impulses to these muscles, and in their consequent contraction. Thus the hand, the foot, the eyes, the speech-organs, etc., may be said to be functionally represented, and in this sense localized, in particular regions of the brain. The same thing is true of the sense-organs, as the eye, ear, etc. Each incoming sensory nerve tract runs to or through some portion of the brain. Injury to this part of the brain results in functional incapacity of the corresponding sense-organ. The cortex, or outer surface of the brain, may thus be conceived as a sort of terminal station for nerves from other portions of the organism, a sort of projection-center which enables them all to take part in a functional unity of action. The functions which can be said in this sense to be localized in the brain are such sensory-motor capacities as the ability to raise the right arm, the ability to balance the body when standing erect with eyes closed, the ability to see, the ability to move the eyeball, the ability to feel pain in a certain area of the skin, the ability to articulate words, to understand spoken or written language, to call up a visual memory of a particular thing previously seen, etc.

The integrity of various parts of the brain is essential to the proper coördination of all the sensibilities and responses of the individual. Traits of character and types of ability, however, depend on the characteristic modes of reaction of the organism as a whole to the factors of its environment. Thus generosity as a human trait does not depend on the massiveness of any set of muscles, nor on the keenness of any sense-organ, but upon the characteristic type of reaction and motivation which the individual as a whole displays. Jealousy, love of children, destructiveness, etc., are characteristic modes of behavior of the whole organism, and depend upon reactions which the given situation evokes, and not upon some special organ.

2. As to the supposed correspondence between size and functional capacity, no evidence has been presented which demonstrates that even the strength of a muscle or the keenness of a sense-organ depends in any way on the absolute size of the brain-area concerned with it. Nor has evidence been presented to prove the existence, within any given species, of correlation between volume, shape, or weight of the brain-tissues and even the more general traits of character or ability. In the absence of such evidence we are led to believe that functional capacity depends on complexity of structure, chemical, molecular, and functional, rather than on the factors of mass or shape. But even the nature of these correlations is as yet largely unknown. The persistence of the faith in the significance of mass and shape probably rests in part on the apparent existence of such correlation when different species are roughly compared with one another. Thus, among the higher vertebrates there seems to be a relation between what we may call the general intelligence of the species and the erect carriage of the body. From the quadrupeds, with their horizontal position, through the apes, with their semiperpendicular mode of life, to the human being, with his erect carriage, there is also a progression in prominence of the forehead, opposition of thumb and finger, relatively greater development of the cerebral mass, and also in mental capacity. The intelligent human being walks in a more erect posture than does the stupid ape. But no one has ventured to assert that a relation exists between erectness of carriage and mental ability when human beings are compared with one another, or when apes are compared with one another. Similarly in the case of the physical features of the brain, the crude relationships which exist empirically, as between different species, seem to be quite slight in significance when compared with the differences in chemical, molecular and functional complexity which are found among

members of the same species. Attempts to discover correlations between mental and moral characteristics and various brain constants we may expect to continue for a long time. What discoveries may be in store for us we do not know. But the important point in the present connection is that, for the purposes of vocational psychology, the practices of phrenology are based on evidence no more relevant to its pretensions than were the "proofs" pointed to by palmistry, horoscopy, and prenatal magic. Through cranial measurements alone it is impossible to determine with certainty the race, age, or sex of an individual, or even, indeed, whether he was a prehistoric savage, an idiot, or a gorilla.

3. As for the third assumption of phrenology, namely, that brain development is reflected in the cranial size or protuberances, it should be sufficient to point out that even if this were so it would be meaningless for our purpose, since we are compelled to abandon the belief in a relation between mass of tissue and even the simplest sensory or motor capacity. But such further disproof as may be required is readily furnished by an actual attempt to remove from their cranial boxes the brains of various animals, and by noting that the shape and thickness of the bones gives little indication as to whether brain tissue, cerebrospinal fluid, or supporting tissues are to be found underneath a given protuberance or depression.

4. The fourth assumption of phrenology, that sparse and casual observation of striking cases is sufficient ground for generalization, we should be able to dismiss at once as utterly inadequate and miscalculated. It is impossible to find consistent recorded instances in which groups of individuals, selected at random, with definitely determined and measured mental or moral characteristics, have been shown to confirm, by their cranial geography, even the most elementary doctrines of that phrenology which still offers to diagnose the individual's psychic constitution and to commend to his future consideration the vocation of engineering, publishing, or preaching, as the case may be. Practicing phrenologists have repeatedly been invited to submit one bit of objective evidence for their pretensions, or to submit themselves to tests under controlled conditions. The invitations are refused, and the inquirer is referred instead to the dogma of some foreign and deceased authority. Such investigations as have been recorded have resulted in negative conclusions, or in contradictory data, or in

coefficients with such high probable errors as to make the figures unreliable.

THE PSEUDO-SCIENCE OF PHYSIOGNOMY

Very often practicing phrenologists and phrenological vocational experts seek to justify their operations and pretensions by pointing out that they do not rely solely on the cranial geography, but more often on other characteristics of the individual's body, such as the concavity or convexity of his profile, the shape of his jaw, the texture of his skin, the shape of his hands, the color of his hair and eyes, the proportions of his trunk, etc. Contemporary vocational counsellors who have enjoyed considerable vogue and commercial repute are especially given to citing these criteria; several recently published tables of these clues are available. Historically, the attempts to formulate principles of physiognomy antedate phrenology by many centuries. Logically, however, physiognomy follows phrenology, as a transition from the formulation of structure to the formulation of behavior. There is a very widespread belief that many mental and moral characteristics betray themselves in special facial items. The shifting eye, lofty brow, massive jaw, thin lips, large ear, protruding or receding chin, dimple, wrinkle, tilted nose, thin skin, prominent veins, and many other characteristics have come, in fiction and in table-talk, to symbolize specific characteristics. The same thing is true of the shuffling gait, the erect body, the protruding paunch, the curved shoulders, enlarged knuckles, stubby or elongated fingers, the short neck, the long arm, and the manner and rate of stride. It is but a step from these to the signs afforded by clothing, its selection, care, and mode of wearing.

Here is indeed a most confused mass of fact and fancy which finds credence in varying degrees on diverse occasions. Seldom has it been analyzed into the definite types of material which it really contains, and its evaluation is commonly left to the haphazard opinion of each individual. There is no doubt that we all tend to form our opinion of a stranger's probable characteristics partly on the basis of these physiognomic, physical, and sartorial factors. To what degree can these items be formulated so as to afford reliable criteria in the analysis of personality, as in the case of vocational selection and employment? We may perhaps best answer this question by noting the various sources of the belief in the validity of physiognomic and similar signs.

1. It is first of all true that many of these marks are the result of habitual activity, and in so far as they originate in the expression of a trait, they may be said to be signs of it. That the studious come to be round-shouldered, the cheerful to have smooth countenances, the guilty to have furtive eye-movements, may well be expected. But it is quite another thing to reverse the proposition and to take stooped shoulders as a universal sign of academic interests, dimples as a sign of guilelessness, and nystagmus as the symptom of a criminal past. It is, however, often safe to use these traits as reliable signs of the established general habits and attitude which they express. We have all done this since earliest childhood; yet any attempt to classify formally the signs and effects of habit and constant expression would be pedantic. Unfortunately for the purposes of vocational guidance of youth, these expressions require for their formation habits of fairly long standing, and the critical period for psychological guidance is likely to be passed long before these settled habits have set the features into their identifiable molds.

Somewhat more hopeful is the reliance on expressive movements as indicative of passing and transient emotional states and attitudes. Not easily can we conceal from the astute observer the momentary passion that may be stirring us. Prolonged intimate acquaintance with an individual's emotional experiences and expressions may in time reveal to such an observer the deeper lying and more permanent affective trends, the moods and sentiments which indicate what we are accustomed to call the temperament of the individual. Insight into the nature of these expressive movements is one of the useful things to be derived from long and patient study of human nature, both at first hand and through the classical descriptions of emotional expression. The more one observes and the more individuals he observes, the more he is impressed with the final variety and informal complexity of these expressive movements, and their dependence on a vast detail of circumstance, which again forbid rule-of-thumb formulation.

2. Another apparent source of these beliefs is in analogy. The clammy hand, the fishy eye, the bull neck, the "blotting paper" voice, the asinine ear, the willowy figure, the feline tread, and scores of such phrases indicate that

these characteristics remind us definitely of various species or objects other than the human being, and that we expect to find back of them the characteristic traits, habits, and instinctive tendencies of those species. We seldom proceed so far as to check up our expectations with facts, under controlled conditions.

3. The affective value of these analogies and their incorporation in poetry, song, and fiction as adequate figures of speech lead us to react to these traits in ways determined largely by the traditional usage. We are humble before the "high-brow," merry in the presence of the dimpled, cautious and prudent before him of the shifting eye. In so far as human reactions are determined by the implied expectations of associates and the demands of immediate circumstances, we should be surprised indeed if the "high-brow" did not, on the strength of his cranium, evade our office-door sentinel, the dimpled one respond to our facetious comment, and he of the shifting eye be forced to steal for a living.

4. Another source of these notions is mainly responsible for such of them as refer to definitely undesirable traits. This is the belief, so well played upon by the school of Lombroso in criminology, that many of these characteristics, along with the so-called physical stigmata, are indicative of a degenerative or atavistic trend in the constitution of the individual. Among these stigmata were enumerated every conceivable extreme variation of every identifiable part of the human anatomy. Lombroso was inclined to believe not only that the presence of such traits was a certain mark of criminal propensities, but even that various types of criminals could be recognized by the cataloging of their stigmata, as thieves, murderers, forgers, etc. The history of the criticism of this view need not be repeated here. Suffice it to say that we now understand that the underlying truth of the matter is only that these stigmata are somewhat more frequent among the vicious, degenerate, and defective groups than they are among people selected on the basis of their morality and intelligence. The criminally inclined individual may possess no stigmata, while an Abraham Lincoln may possess several of them, and in marked degree. To be sure, when an unusual number of stigmata are presented by an individual, we feel disposed to suspect that the abnormal condition is not confined to his bones and peripheral organs alone, but is probably so deep-seated as to involve his nervous system as well. But on the basis of these stigmata alone we are

quite unable to decide whether he is an imbecile, a degenerate criminal, a pervert, a genius, or only an average man, with an undue burden of physical infirmity; still less can we diagnose his special mental or moral qualities.

5. A further source of these physiognomic beliefs may be discerned: namely, the fact that the features of a stranger are very likely to call more or less clearly to our memory some other acquaintance whose traits we know, to our sorrow perhaps, and whose features or manner or voice or apparel chance to be very similar to that of the stranger. At once we are inclined to endow the stranger with the character of the individual he resembles. We seldom accurately check up these impressions on the basis of subsequent discovery. Indeed we are much more likely to evoke the suspected traits by our own attitude and by our treatment of the stranger, and we are eager to pounce upon any act that may be construed as a confirmation of our snap judgment. It is obvious that these impressions will vary from individual to individual and that any attempt to formulate them would expose their fallaciousness.

6. Finally, in this analysis of the origin of our belief in the signs of physiognomy, is the mere insistence that as a matter of fact there are definite relationships discoverable and formulable between typical features and typical characteristics of personality. Beliefs of this dogmatic kind are most likely to be exploited by the professional counsellor, since they appear to the examinee to be unknown, mysterious, esoteric facts. The following formulations, taken from an account of the performance of one of the most widely advertised of professional vocational counsellors, may serve as an example of this type of dogmatic physiognomic doctrine.

"The sensitive, delicate-minded man usually has a fine-textured skin; the coarse-minded man a coarse-textured skin. It is an embryological fact that the skin was and is the original seat of all sensations, and that spinal cords and nerves are but modified and specialized in-turned skin. Of necessity a man's skin indicates the texture of his brain.

"Texture is a great classifier of humanity. The individual of fine hair, fine-textured skin, delicately chiseled features, slender, graceful body and limbs, as a general rule, is refined, loves beauty and grace, and likes work either purely mental in its nature or offering an opportunity to handle fine, delicate materials and tools. On the other hand the man with coarse hair, coarse-textured skin, and large, strongly formed features inclines as a general rule to occupations in which strength, vigor, virility, and ability to live and work in the midst of harsh, rough and unbeautiful conditions are prime requirements.

"It is no secret to observant employers of labor that blondes, as a general rule, are changeable, variety loving, optimistic, and speculative, while brunettes are consistent, steady, dependable, serious, and conservative."

"It turns out as one might naturally expect that the man who resembles the greyhound in form is quicker, keener, more responsive, and less enduring than the man who resembles the bulldog in form.

"A most cursory examination of the portraits of poets, educators, and essayists will show a marked tendency in them to resemble the triangle in structure of the head and body—both head and body wide above and narrower in the lower portions. An examination of the portraits of a hundred great generals, pioneers, builders, engineers, explorers, athletes, automobile racers, aëronauts, and others who lead a life of great activity will show a general tendency toward structure on the lines of the square—square face, square body, square hands. Reference to the portraits of great judges, financiers, organizers, and commercial kings will show a general tendency toward structure upon the lines of the circle—round face, rounded body and a tendency to roundness in hands and limbs.

"Anything which is hard in consistency has comparatively great resistance and persistence. That which is elastic in consistency is adaptable and seems to have spring, life, and energy within it. These principles have been found to apply to human beings."

The existence of quite definite beliefs in these relations between character and physiognomy is readily shown by experiments in which groups of ten people were asked to arrange twenty photographs of women in an order of merit. On different occasions and by varying groups of mature college students, these photographs were arranged on the basis of seven different traits, viz.: intelligence, humor, perseverance, kindness, conceit, courage, and deceitfulness. Different judges show quite striking agreement in their estimates of the characteristics suggested by a given photograph. Thus, if the average position assigned to each photograph be taken as the standard and the divergences of the ten judges from this standard be averaged in the case of all the photographs, the average divergences for the different traits are as follows[2]:

Intelligence 2.86 places
Perseverance 3.32 "
Kindliness 3.55 "
Conceit 3.57 "
Courage 3.69 "
Humor 3.90 "
Deceitfulness 4.14 "

This means that in the long run a stranger will place a given individual in a group of twenty persons not over three or four positions away from the place to which other strangers would assign him. The individual's physiognomy, however little it may actually reveal of his personality, nevertheless suggests rather definite characteristics to those whom he meets, and to that degree determines their reaction toward him, expectations of him, and belief in him. The definiteness or agreement of these impressions seems also to vary with the trait in question; it is high for intelligence and perseverance, low for humor and deceitfulness, and intermediate for kindliness, conceit, and courage. Our own results, however, must be taken only as suggestive, rather than as general, since they may easily have been determined partly by the particular set of photographs we used and by our particular and diverse sets of judges.[3]

Results of this character, and many similar ones which we are accumulating, suggest, however, an interesting set of problems. It is psychologically as interesting to inquire just what impressions people actually receive from one's physiognomy and expression, as it is to ask whether these impressions are correct. One's ultimate vocational accomplishment often depends on the first impression he creates, the type of reception his appearance invites, even though there may be no necessary connection whatever between appearance and mental constitution. Vocational success depends not only on the traits one really possesses, but also somewhat on the traits one is believed to possess.

It is also interesting to observe that high correlations exist between some of the traits as judged merely on the basis of photographs. Let 1.00 be taken to indicate complete correspondence between two orders of merit, so that the highest in the one scale is also the highest in the other scale, the second in one the second in the other, and so on; then -1.00 will indicate a completely reversed order, the best in one class being the poorest in the other, etc.; a coefficient of 0 will mean only a chance relationship, i. e., none at all. Then from 1.00 through 0 to -1.00 we have represented all possible degrees of correspondence.[4] These figures are called "coefficients of correlation," and can easily be computed by proper statistical methods. In the present case the coefficients for all combinations of two traits are as follows:

	Intelligence	Humor	Perseverance	Kindliness	Conceit	Courage
Humor	.47					
Perseverance	.88	.33				
Kindliness	.76	.65	.39			
Conceit	.28	-.03	.08	-.56		
Courage	.89	.43	.79	.72	-.25	
Deceitfulness	-.11	-.28	-.02	-.69	.66	-.49

It will be seen that the intelligent, humorous, persevering, kindly, and courageous countenances tend to be the same ones, and that the faces suggesting the opposites or low degrees of these traits also tend to be very much the same ones. This is indicated by the high positive coefficients between these traits. But conceit and deceitfulness show negative or very low positive correlation with all traits except each other. In this latter case the correlation is positive and high (.66). Other interesting relations between these judgments of character can be inferred from the table of coefficients. But it should be remembered that we are not here dealing with traits as demonstrably present, but only as judged on the basis of facial characteristics and expression. The actual relation between the physiognomic details and the true character of the individual displaying them is a totally different matter. The close correlations between the several desirable traits and between the several undesirable traits, as found in this table of coefficients, seem to have a further significance and suggest that the observers do not judge each trait on the basis of particular and specific physiognomic details. They seem, rather, to get a general impression of favorableness or unfavorableness, and to rank the photographs on the basis of this general impression, no matter which trait is being judged.

It is a common practice for employers, superintendents, agencies, etc., to request the applicant for a position to send his or her photograph for inspection. The urgency of some of these requests and the emphasis placed on them seem to indicate that the photograph is believed to be valuable not only for its service in revealing the general features but also for some further and more specific indications which it affords. Very few attempts seem to have been made to test actually the value of judgments of character when they are based on photographs rather than on acquaintance. Experiments recently conducted yield some interesting preliminary data on this question. The question proposed was: "What relation exists between the judgments which strangers form, on the basis of an individual's photograph, and the judgments which acquaintances make on the basis of daily familiarity and long observation?"[5]

All the members of a group of college women were judged by twenty-four of their associates, for a number of more or less definite characteristics. The twenty-five individuals constituting the group were arranged in an order of merit for each trait, by each of the twenty-four judges. Only one arrangement, for one trait, was made by any one judge within a given week. The judgments were thus distributed over a considerable interval so that judgments for one trait might influence as slightly as possible the judgments of later traits. All these twenty-four judgments were then averaged for each trait, and the final position of each person in each trait thus determined by the consensus of opinion of the judges. This measure is then a combined estimate on the basis of actual conduct and behavior.

Photographs of all the members of the group were then secured, all of them taken by the same photographer, in the same style and size. These photographs were now judged, by a group of twenty-five men and a group of twenty-five women, all of whom were *totally unacquainted* with the individuals who were being judged. These strangers arranged the photographs in order of merit for the various traits of character, just as the earlier group of judges had arranged the names of the members of the group, with all of whom they were acquainted. The various arrangements of the photographs were then averaged, yielding for each photograph an average position in each trait. We thus have three measures of the group of college women: (1) the judgments of their intimate associates; (2) the judgments of twenty-five men, on the basis of photographs, and (3) the judgments of twenty-five women, on the basis of photographs. All of these measures may be compared with each other, and correlated so as to show their respective amounts of correspondence. The results are as follows:

Trait	Judgments by Associates Compared with the Judgments of the Photographs		
	By 25 Men	By 25 Women	Average
Neatness	.03	.07	.05
Conceit	.10	.27	.19
Sociability	.29	.29	.29
Humor	.21	.45	.33
Likeability	.30	.45	.38
Intelligence	.42	.61	.51
Refinement	.50	.52	.51
Beauty	.60	.49	.55
Snobbishness	.58	.53	.56
Vulgarity	.61	.69	.65
Average	.36	.43	.40

The correspondence between judgments of acquaintance and judgments of photographs is seen to vary with the trait in question. Such traits as neatness, conceit, sociability, humor, and likeability, important as they are for vocational success or failure, show very low correlation. The judgments of the photographs tell almost nothing at all of the nature of the impression which the individual makes on her acquaintances, her true character. With the remaining traits—beauty, intelligence, refinement, snobbishness, and vulgarity—the coefficients are considerably larger, and suggest that the photographs tend to be judged by the strangers in somewhat the same way as the individuals are judged by their acquaintances.

Two points of special importance should be noted in this connection. The first is that these correlations are not between the judgments of single individuals. It is the combined or group judgment of twenty-five judges which is required to yield these coefficients which even then average only about .40 correlation with the estimates of associates. The following table shows the ability of ten judges, chosen at random, to estimate these characteristics through the examination of the photographs. In securing this table the arrangement made by each individual judge was correlated with the established order as determined by the estimates of associates, in the case of the three traits—intelligence, neatness and sociability.

Judge	Individual Correctness of Judges in Estimating		
	Intelligence	Neatness	Sociability
I	.51	.11	.39
II	.11	.10	.08
III	.15	.29	.05
IV	-.27	.06	.49
V	.08	.24	.08
VI	.43	.41	.28
VII	.04	.11	.02
VIII	.39	-.09	.32
IX	.22	-.08	.00
X	.30	.02	.55
Average	.19	.11	.22

These random samples of individual judicial capacity show at once how unreliable individual judgment is in these matters. The individual judges vary widely among themselves and they also depart widely from the established order. Moreover, a judge who may happen to show a reasonable degree of correctness in judging sociability may be very far away from correctness in judging the other traits, or may, indeed, judge in quite the reverse of the correct order. To have accepted the verdicts of a single judge would not only have been manifestly unfair to the individual but also hazardous to the employer. The combined impressions of twenty-five judges is here required for the correlations for even half of the traits to reach over .38.

The second point to be noted is that even under these circumstances the coefficients are far from perfect, even for those traits in which they are the highest. Only if beauty, snobbishness, or vulgarity are the traits which are crucial, are judgments of the photographs reliable enough to be worth considering. It would appear that the vocations which depend markedly on these characteristics are exceedingly few. And even here, although the reliance on coefficients of .55 might in all probability aid the employer in decreasing the percentage of the snobbish or the vulgar among his employees, grave injustice would most certainly be done to those many individuals who constitute exceptions and keep the correlations from being perfect. Only when correlation coefficients are very high can their indications be applied in the guidance of individuals (as distinguished from the selection of groups) with safety and justice.

Dean Schneider reports an attempt to verify the principles of a certain system of physiognomics by putting them to an actual test. He writes:

"A group in the scientific management field affirmed that an examination of physical characteristics such as the shape of the fingers and shape of the head, disclosed aptitudes and abilities. For example, a directive, money-making executive will have a certain shaped head and hand. A number of money-making executives were picked at random and their physical characteristics charted. We do not find that they conform at all to any law. Also we found men who had the physical characteristics that ought to make them executives, but they were anything but executives. A number of tests of this kind gave negative results. We were forced to the conclusion that this system was not reliable."

We must content ourselves on this point by insisting that the formulated facts of physiognomy are so unsupported, contradictory, and extravagant that the vocational psychologist cannot afford to trifle with them. General impressions on the basis of the totality of an individual's appearance, bearing, and behavior we shall always tend to receive. Whether one judges more accurately by an analytic recording of each detail or by ignoring these in favor of his own more or less unanalyzed total impression has never been demonstrated. Under any circumstances one is likely to look about for such details as may lend support to the total impression. But it is quite unjustifiable—though perhaps commercially expedient—to pretend that the judgment is really based on the details selected.

The life of him who bases his expectations of human conduct on the physiognomy of his neighbors is bound to be full of delightful as well as fearful surprises. I shall never forget the practical lesson in the principles of physiognomics I learned when watching a shipload of immigrants pass the physical and mental examinations at Ellis Island. Admission to the new land, and to the theater of their vocational plans, depended on the results of these examinations. Ellis Island is perhaps the one place in the world where principles of individual psychology are most in demand, and where such principles as are relied on lead to results of the most serious human consequences. I watched the line file past the preliminary gate, by the inspectors who scrutinized them still more carefully, and on into the inner room where the suspected ones were submitted to more searching examination. One young woman stood out among her companions as easily the most comely and attractive of the women. She was the only one of that shipload who was finally certified as an imbecile, and refused admission to the mainland.

The physiognomic analyses, then, do not merit serious consideration as instruments of vocational guidance and selection. The mere facts of physical structure, contour, shape, texture, proportion, color, etc., yield no more information concerning capacities and interests than did the incantations of the primitive medicine-man or the absurd charts of the phrenologists. In so far as character and ability may be determined by facts of structure, it is by the minute structure of the microscopic elements of the brain and other vital tissues, about which we now know exceedingly little. We shall therefore dismiss from further consideration the futile attempts to diagnose mental constitution on the basis of bodily structure, and turn to the more reliable and scientifically conceived methods of inferring the individual's mental traits from his behavior or his actual performance when tests are made under controlled conditions.

FOOTNOTES:

[1] An interesting review of the origin and development of phrenology and other systems of character analysis is given by Joseph Jastrow, in an article in *Popular Science Monthly*, June, 1915.

[2] To make clear the way in which these figures are secured, and to show concretely what they mean, suppose that the twenty photographs are lettered A, B, C, D, etc. They are to be arranged in an order by each judge according to his judgment of the intelligence of the individuals, the individuals being unknown to the judges. Suppose that the ten judges place photograph A respectively in the following positions: 9, 11, 5, 8, 9, 12, 7, 8, 7, 14. The average of these ten positions is 9, which we then take as the standard or most probable position of photograph A. Only two of the judges actually place A in the ninth position. The other eight judges all vary more or less from this position. We then find how much each judge varies from the average of the group, and the ten variations are respectively 0, 2, 4, 1, 0, 3, 2, 1, 2, 5 positions. The average of these individual

variations is 2.0 positions. This figure indicates how closely the ten judges agree in their estimates of photograph A, a small average deviation indicating close agreement. In this way we find for each of the twenty photographs its average deviation; and if the twenty figures thus secured are in their turn averaged we secure an approximate measure of the disagreement of the judges when estimating the intelligence suggested by the photographs. Similarly we may compute average deviations for any other trait which is judged. These final figures are the ones which are given in the table, each of them being the average of twenty photographs as judged by ten persons.

[3] In such experiments the actual magnitude of the measure of variation becomes larger as the number of judges is reduced, the number of photographs increased, or the photographs so selected as to resemble one another more closely.

[4] Since such coefficients of correlation will be frequently used throughout the book as measures of the amount of correspondence or relationship between two things, it may be well at this point to indicate briefly how they are computed. Suppose that, as arranged in order on the basis of their final averages, the photographs stand in the following positions for the two traits—courage and kindliness.

Photo	Courage	Kindliness	d	d^2
A	2	5	3	9
B	5	1	4	16
C	10	13	3	9
D	1	4	3	9
E	7	6	1	1
F	11	8	3	9
G	14	10	4	16
H	20	15	5	25
I	16	12	4	16
J	4	2	2	4
K	8	14	6	36
L	3	3	0	0
M	12	20	8	64
N	15	11	4	16
O	17	18	1	1
P	9	7	2	4
Q	6	17	9	81

When the several values under d^2 are added their sum is 376. This, multiplied by 6, according to the formula, gives 2256. The denominator of the fraction is, since there are 20 cases, 7980. Dividing 2256 by 7980 gives us .28; for 7980 is 20 times 399, which in turn is 202—1. When this is subtracted from 1.00 it gives us .72, which is the measure of correlation between the two orders. Since it is very high it suggests that

R	13	9	4	16	the two traits are judged
S	18	16	2	4	in much the same way.
T	19	19	0	0	

A formula is provided by mathematicians which enables us to compute the degree of resemblance between these two orders. There are, in fact, several formulae for such purposes, all of which yield substantially the same results. The one used in this case was $r = 1.00 - (6\Sigma d^2)/(n(n^2-1))$. In this formula r stands for the coefficient of correlation for which we are working; d is the difference between the positions which each of the photographs receives in the two traits; Σ means the sum of these differences when each has been squared or multiplied by itself; n means the number of cases, which is in this case 20, since there are that number of photographs. When these substitutions are made and the equation solved, the result will be the measure of resemblance, which will lie somewhere between +1.00 and -1.00, as explained in the text. This calculation is carried out here for the two sample traits, for the convenience of readers who may not be familiar with statistical methods.

[5] These experiments were conducted by Lucy G. Cogan, M. A., to whom I am indebted for permission to use the results in advance of their more detailed publication in her forthcoming paper on "Judgments of Character on the Basis of Photographs."

CHAPTER III

THE DEVELOPMENT OF PSYCHOLOGICAL TESTS

ORIGIN AND HISTORY OF TESTS

Barren as phrenology and physiognomics were of formulable and useful results, they nevertheless served the purpose of directing attention toward the study of individual differences in mental characteristics as a distinct branch of inquiry. The next step consisted in the semi-experimental plan of observing the individual's *behavior* under a variety of uncontrolled circumstances or on more carefully planned occasions, in the endeavor to secure more or less exact quantitative expressions of the degree to which he displayed certain types of ability. Underlying the various abilities and involved in them there were assumed to lie a limited number of faculties or powers of the mind. Each individual was conceived to possess much the same faculties, but in varying degrees or amounts or forms. Attention, memory, apperception, reasoning, will, feeling, etc., were the fundamental "faculties"; and differences in character were thought of as depending upon the varying amounts and interrelations of these fundamental faculties. In the endeavor to discover types of experiment which would measure these "faculties" it was found, in time, that a given "faculty" did not appear, on close examination, to be as unitary as it was formerly supposed to be. It was seen that to have a good memory for one kind of material did not at once signify a good memory for every sort of thing. Determination in one direction did not imply the general quality of resoluteness. It began to be realized that attention, memory, discrimination, and the other "faculties" are very much more highly specialized than these general names indicate. The unitary soul had early been split up into the list of "faculties" or categories, and now these in turn came each to be split up into finer and finer aptitudes and tendencies, until, in the radical reaction of recent years, we find the human mind described as made up of an infinite number of independent connections or bonds between more or less specific stimulus and more or less definite response. The old "faculties" came now to be looked on as descriptive terms for certain rather general and abstracted characteristics of these multitudinous and detailed reaction tendencies, rather than as in themselves agents or powers or forces, as they were formerly conceived.

During this change in theoretical description and continuing into our present era of compromise and revision, methods were developed of measuring the amount and quality, or, more simply conceived, the speed, strength and regularity of mental and motor ability. Beginning in the form of experiments on sensory discrimination, reaction time and imagery type, and combined with physiological measurements of motor strength, rapidity and fatigue, these experiments developed, in certain hands, into what are now known as "mental tests." Since the principle and method of mental and physical tests is the chief characteristic of the present status of vocational psychology, and since the work of the immediate future seems destined to develop mainly in this same direction, we may profitably consider at this point the history and development of the mental test. We may later take up the general principle and theory of the test as an instrument of psychological analysis and diagnosis, with special reference to the requirements and implications of such tests as may be of service in vocational psychology. We shall then be in position to review the special vocational tests that have as yet been proposed, to evaluate their outstanding results, and to point to some of the more immediate prospects and problems under consideration by those interested in the application of psychological tests in vocational analysis and guidance.

We may begin with an account of the first definite attempt to explore systematically the personality of individuals by the method of tests. The "Columbia Freshman Tests" are of especial interest in the history of vocational psychology, since in their formulation and plan explicit thought was given to the practical use to which the results of tests might be put by the individuals examined, and by the statistical study of the results by students of the subject. In 1894, under the guidance of Professor Cattell, there was instituted the plan of testing the students of Columbia College during their first and fourth academic years. A description of the tests employed was published by Cattell and Farrand in 1896, and a statistical study of results was published by Wissler in 1901.

The motive back of these tests is well expressed in the following paragraph which was also used as material for a test of logical memory:

"Tests such as we are now making are of value both for the advancement of science and for the information of the student who is tested. It is of importance for science to learn how people differ and on what factors these differences depend. If we can disentangle the complex influences of heredity and environment we may be able to apply our knowledge to guide human development. Then it is well for each of us to know in what way he differs from others. We may thus in some cases correct defects and develop aptitudes which we might otherwise neglect."

The nature of these Columbia tests and the method of recording and reporting them are indicated in the forms which were printed and used for this special purpose. (Samples of these are given in the Appendix.) They are given here not so much for the sake of the enumeration of the tests, since many of these are no longer in common use, but because of their historic interests for vocational psychology and because of the general plan outlined in them. In general this plan is that of accumulating measurements of a large number of individuals and thus showing each one how he compares with the normal or average, or where he stands in the general curve of distribution of the members of the group. These tests were applied to the same individuals on their entrance to and their graduation from college, in order to indicate changes that might have been made during the intervening period.

Especially interesting also are other blanks containing additional data, such as age, health, physical characteristics, physiognomic features, enumeration of stigmata, etc. In addition to the tests and measurements, the examiner, both before and after the interview, recorded his general impression of the individual, in the terms indicated on the blank form. We shall have occasion to refer to these judgments of general impression in more detail when we come to consider the use of the interview and the testimonial in vocational psychology. Account was also taken of the gymnasium records of the student, as to nationality, birth, parentage, habits, health, etc.

The Columbia tests may be thought of as representative of several similar projects developed in this country and in Germany, France and England by many workers. The names of Galton, Cattell, Kraepelin, Binet, Henri, and Jastrow stand out conspicuously in the early history of mental tests. The first step was thus the invention, description and trial of a great number of miscellaneous tests, with little analysis of the tests themselves, the nature of the functions tested by them, or their relation to each other. Aside from the strictly motor and physical tests those devised were mainly of so-called intellectual character: measurements of speed and accuracy with which certain definite tasks could be accomplished. They were, moreover, very simple in character, not necessarily related to the work of daily life, with only a single or but a few trials made on each individual. Tests of affective and volitional factors were slower in developing. Little account was taken of interests, instinctive and emotional characteristics, attitudes, adaptation, methods of attack, limits of ability after practice, or many other aspects of individuality which later work has shown to be important.

The next step in the development of tests consisted in the coöperative effort to standardize the nature and methods, the conditions and mode of record. Many hands had part in this process, until in recent years, through publication, comparison and discussion of the subject, fairly uniform principles of technique, record, and treatment of measures have been agreed upon. This made possible the comparison of results secured by different investigators, and facilitated the statistical treatment of the data, so that later work might profit by what had already been tried or accomplished by earlier workers. After many years of this sort of coöperative work, another series of studies was inaugurated to attempt what has come to be known as "testing the tests." These studies proceeded by examining into the degree to which the various tests correlate with each other, with other indications of the individual's ability, with age, sex, health, education, school standing, special training, etc. Such questions as the following will suggest the problems involved in "testing the tests."

1. Which of the various tests correlate with each other?

2. What correlation exists between mental and motor abilities?

3. Do the tests measure fundamental qualities or general powers of the individual, or specialized capacities, or perhaps mainly the effect of general or special training?

4. If they measure general qualities, which of the existing tests are the best for this purpose?

5. How many trials are needed to afford a reliable index of the individual's ability?

6. What are the principal incidental factors that influence the result of tests?

7. Which tests are most easily influenced or disturbed by extraneous factors?

8. Can tests of the simpler laboratory type be used to indicate the individual's ability as shown in his daily work and play?

9. How simple or complex should the various tests be in order to give the best results?

10. How many tests, and which, are required to give a fairly correct picture of the individual's psychological make-up?

11. To what degree do preliminary trials indicate the final capacity of an individual?

12. Does the intercorrelation of tests change in any way with practice, repetition, and familiarity with the material?

13. Just what mental functions may the particular tests be said to measure?

14. How important are these functions in practical, educational and vocational life?

15. By what amounts and in what various ways do individuals differ among themselves in such abilities as the tests measure?

16. Are there other important aspects of psychological constitution and equipment for which there now exist no adequate tests?

The investigation of these numerous problems has resulted in the accumulation of a considerable literature of mental tests. Many of the earlier forms of tests were abandoned because of their unsatisfactory or meaningless character. Others have been retained and improved in form, and many new ones are constantly being devised and elaborated, described and standardized. The precautions to be observed, the instructions to be given, and the methods of record and interpretation have been presented in various books and manuals. The tests have been developed for more and more complex functions, and now relate not only to relatively simple capacities but to highly elaborate and subtle forms of achievement. As rapidly as is consistent with accuracy, norms and standards of performance for different ages, school grades, vocational requirements, etc., are being accumulated and reported. Typical charts of age norms in selected tests are given in the Appendix.

As the tests have thus developed they have been organized for a variety of special purposes, such as for school measurement, educational diagnosis, clinical examination, laboratory experiment, and more recently for the purposes of vocational guidance and selection. Among the first of these to develop systematically, and also the ones with the most immediate vocational application, are the graded intelligence scales, which shall be our next concern.

GRADED INTELLIGENCE SCALES AND NORMS

An important step in the history of general tests is represented by the accumulation of norms and standards of performance for the different selected tests, and the arrangement of scales of tests with increasing difficulty, as further aids in fixing the individual's status.

After a standardized and tested form of test has been selected, norms of performance are accumulated by applying the test to large numbers of persons of the same general type. The classification may be on the basis of age, school grade, occupation, nationality, etc. In this way it becomes possible to determine for a given individual how he compares with other members of his group; whether he is above or below the average, and how far; whether he would belong among the best ten, or the poorest ten, or the third ten, etc., of one hundred selected at random. Such norms also reveal to what degree the tested ability varies with the other factors, on the basis of which the group was selected, as age, sex, education, size, health, race, etc.

As rapidly as reliable norms are established, it becomes possible to select for each age, school grade, occupation, etc., a set of tests which the average person of that age, schooling or calling should be able to perform to a certain known degree of proficiency. Failure to accomplish this indicates performance lower than that expected and in so far as success is dependent solely on mental ability, indicates inferior capacity. Similarly, ability to do more than the average or normal record requires indicates a capacity that is precocious, rare, and superior.

In this way are derived standard graded scales which represent a decided advance in the science of psychological diagnosis. There are three rather different forms in which attempts have been made to secure such scales. In one form the scale consists of a series of steps, each step consisting of different sorts of performance; that is, different tests or tasks are used. These tasks are arranged in groups, each group representing tests which should be passed acceptably by individuals of the given age, school grade, etc. In another form of scale the type of task is the same throughout, but the different points on the scale are represented by increasingly difficult specimens of material. The scale thus presents graded steps of difficulty in doing the same general sort of thing. In the third form the task remains precisely the same throughout, and performance is measured in terms of the time in which the task can be completed and the accuracy which is displayed. Sometimes, in scales of this type, although the instructions are always the same, the test is performed with varying degrees of approximation to a qualitative standard, and the steps may then consist of these graded qualitative achievements.

As representative of the first form of scale we may refer to the widely used Binet-Simon scale for the determination of mental age. Whatever we mean by intelligence, it is a characteristic which is essential to vocational activity. It is furthermore a characteristic which normally tends to increase in its degree or manifestation from infancy up to at least ten or twelve years of age. Beyond that point there are, to be sure, striking individual differences in that characteristic which we call intelligence, but beyond this point it does not seem so dependent on the physical age of the organism. Five-year-old children tend to be pretty much alike in intelligence. At least, the change from five years to seven years is commonly attended by very apparent growth in this respect, and a five-year-old is more like other five-year-olds in the things he can do than he is like seven-year-olds.

Experiment and observation show that the ages up to ten or twelve tend to indicate rather definite mental status, in the long run, although, to be sure, children of a given age vary considerably from one another. But beyond this point the age of an individual is not by any means an indication of the sort or degree of ability to be expected of him. The further we go beyond this point, the less significant becomes the mere statement of the individual's age. We may thus indicate the mental attainment of a child of less than twelve years by stating the average age of children who can do the things, know the facts, display the abilities that he can. This figure we will use to indicate his *mental* age as distinguished from his *chronological* or *physical* or *actual age.* A record-blank which enumerates the tests comprising the Binet-Simon scale is given in the Appendix. Those who may be interested in using this or similar scales should familiarize themselves with some of the many books and manuals that have been written concerning them, the methods of using them, their characteristic results and their evaluation. These scales will be again considered in a later section, when we discuss the measures of general intelligence as they relate to vocational guidance and selection.

Other scales than the Binet-Simon series have been proposed, and this series has itself undergone modifications at the hands of later investigators—changes calculated to render it more reliable and adaptable. Much work is now being done in the attempt to develop scales or sets of tests which will reveal characteristic differences among people whose mentality has gone beyond the point which the juvenile scales reach.

The work of Trabue in standardizing the "completion test" so that individuals may be quantitatively compared on the basis of it may serve as an example of the second form of scale. This particular test consists in requiring the individual to supply meaningful words or phrases in the blank spaces formed by mutilating logical text. It is similar to the simple exercise sometimes found in elementary text books of grammar and spelling. It seems that the ability to supply the missing words or phrases quickly in such mutilated material calls for the exercise of a type of ability which correlates to a high degree with most other measures of intelligence. Individual differences as shown by school grades, age, opinion of teachers, estimates of associates, results of other mental tests, etc., are readily and with considerable reliability revealed in the individual's ability to perform this type of test. This investigator has, after much preliminary labor, constructed a form of this test in which the material gradually increases in difficulty from beginning to end. Efficiency in the test may be measured by the point one can reach in the text in a given time. This test has been standardized, not on the basis of physical age, as in the case of the Binet-Simon scale, but on the basis of school grade, from the second grade through the high school, some four or six years beyond the point where the Binet-Simon scale ceases to be useful. A copy of this test is also given in the Appendix. Those who wish to use it should consult the original description of it, for technique, precautions, norms, and interpretation.

A good example of the third form of scale is to be found in Sylvester's standardization of the "form-board" test. The "form-board" is one of the most useful tests in detecting intellectual defect that is so pronounced as to constitute the individual a "mental defective." Out of a solid base board are cut various geometrical forms, such as diamonds, stars, squares, triangular blocks, etc. These blocks are placed alongside the base from which they have been cut. The task is that of replacing all the blocks in their appropriate places, with the greatest possible speed. The test tends to reveal characteristic defects in understanding instructions, perceiving the general and specific situations, profiting by experience, recognizing form and size and other space relations, etc. The individual may work blind-folded or may use his eyes.

In the standardized form the sizes, shapes and positions are uniformly adopted and the technique of instruction and procedure is specified. Under these conditions the time required to complete the task by normal children of the ages five to fourteen years has been recorded. Sylvester presents a curve based on the examination of 1,537 normal children. The curve shows the average time of performance for each age and also indicates the range of performance for each age. In the case of a given individual it is thus easy, by referring to the standard table of norms, to determine whether he is up to the normal record for his age, whether he is within the normal range of variation for this age, and how deficient or precocious he may be in this respect. Tables of this type are now being accumulated for a great variety of single standard tests.

In addition to scales of this type, which proceed by setting for the individual a graded series of tasks and determining his success in their accomplishment, there is a further type of graded scale which is now represented by several standard specimens. This is the type of scale which is designed to afford an instrument for the measurement of such products as the actual work of the individual incidentally yields. Thorndike's "Scale for the Measurement of Handwriting" is the model on which many of the later scales of this type have been based. In this scale actual specimens of handwriting are arranged in a graduated series in such a way that the steps from specimen to specimen are equally appreciable or noticeable, and in this sense uniform. When such a scale extends from an actual zero point, it is possible to "measure" the quality of handwriting in quite the same way as that in which one measures the height of an individual or the length of a table. The quantitative measure consists in the statement of the number of stages which intervene between that quality of product represented by the specimen and the zero point of the scale. The position assigned to the specimen being measured is determined by moving the specimen along the graded series of standards until a point is reached where the specimen seems, on the basis of direct inspection, to belong. Such scales have been formulated for various special forms of school work, such as handwriting, drawing, arithmetic, literary composition, mechanical construction, etc. By such means it is possible not only to measure the "general intelligence" of the worker, but also his actual ability in creating a definite type of product. There seems to be no limit to the possibilities of scales of this form, and their value in determining the more definite and particular capacities, whether from the point of view of original endowment or from the point of view of the effects of training, is obvious.

These various scales for measuring general intelligence have been used chiefly for the purposes of educational diagnosis, in determining the degree of backwardness of children in the grades, their need for special educational attention, or the hopelessness of further pedagogical effort with them. But it is obvious at once that tests of this type are of great use to an employer in eliminating, from among the candidates for work, those who are hopelessly mentally defective, feeble-minded, and irresponsible. There are many sorts of work in which the employment of feeble-minded persons, unrecognizable as such by their physical traits or by a casual inspection, not only entails loss and annoyance but may constitute a positive danger and constant menace to those who rely on the defective individual. Such work as that of delivery boys, messengers, domestic servants, nurses, elevator operators, drivers, motormen, etc., may be cited as instances of work into which the feeble-minded easily slip, unless there is some standardized means of recognizing them.

The importance of detecting these incompetents and keeping them from work in which their irresponsibility means economic waste and personal and social danger is of distinct vocational interest. Studies of cases brought to the Clearing House for Mental Defectives in New York City show that of the first two hundred and eighty-one feeble-minded women of child-bearing age, about two-thirds had been engaged in some form of economic labor in which their incompetence was distinctly dangerous to those associated with them. The following table shows how these two hundred and eighty-one feeble-minded women had been employed:

Living at home and assisting at simple tasks	94
Domestic service (families, bars, hotels, etc.)	67
Engaged in factory operations	21
Living in institutions, reformatories, asylums	20
Prostitutes	30
Laundresses	5
Working in stores, clerking, errands, etc.	5
Nursemaids	9
Odd jobs	6
Married and keeping house	11
Housework, with relatives	13

The investigators originally reporting these data write as follows: "These defective women had borne eighty-nine illegitimate children, which were acknowledged and could be somewhat definitely located, and sixteen women were illegitimately pregnant at the time of their examination at the Clearing House. Twenty-four of the two hundred and eighty-one had married and these had borne forty-six legitimate children. The average mental age of the illegitimate mothers was nine years."

The employment of feeble-minded women as domestics, factory operatives, laundresses, clerks, and nursemaids constitutes not only a nuisance to the general public, but a real source of inefficiency and danger to the community. Graded scales for the measurement of intelligence will have amply repaid the labor devoted to their formulation if they aid us in the proper segregation and vocational supervision of the mentally defective. The feeble-minded boy is more likely to be observed in the natural course of things, because of the more strictly competitive types of work into which boys customarily go, but it is far from realized how much loss of property, life, and general happiness is entailed upon the community by the indiscriminate employment of untested boys and men as floating employees.

But the vocational value of the graded intelligence scales and norms is not limited to the work of detecting and eliminating the feeble-minded. Many of the tests as now standardized yield measures of intelligence, capacity and comprehension ranging far above the level which constitutes the borderline of mental defect. Some of them reach somewhat higher than the average intelligence and capacity of the college freshman. It is thus possible, through the use of the graded scales, to measure in quantitative terms the general intelligence as well as various more special capacities of applicants and candidates for positions for which general intelligence is the chief requisite. Such tests are now used in many places in the selection of clerical workers, telephone operators, stenographers, waitresses, motormen, salesmen, office help, inspectors, watchmen, soldiers, and special types of factory workers. Thus Trabue reports a study in which Professor Scott tested thirty efficiency experts employed by a large industrial concern in New England. Ten psychological tests were used, including a completion test. The men were also judged on the basis of their relative abilities by the members of the firm. The combined tests correlated with the combined judgments, giving the very high coefficient of .87. The completion test alone yielded a coefficient of .64. From the point of view of vocational selection we may expect the principle of the graded intelligence scale to become increasingly valuable as more and more norms are established. The first definite contribution of vocational psychology is thus not so much toward the guidance of the individual worker as for the guidance of the employer who may be required to select from a number of applicants those whose general intellectual equipment is most adequate. But we shall later have occasion to point out a further contribution which this makes possible, in so far as it may enable us to classify the operations involved in various types of work and to align these operations and tasks along the general intelligence scale. Such alignment will enable us to specify the approximate degree of general intelligence which a given position demands, and thus, in the case of the simpler tasks, afford a means of vocational guidance as well as vocational selection.

CHAPTER IV

THE PSYCHOGRAPHIC METHODS

THE INDIVIDUAL PSYCHOGRAPH

Another application of mental tests has a very direct interest for vocational psychology. This is the method of the "psychograph," as it is commonly called. The French and German psychologists especially have been active in advocating the practice of submitting to careful and detailed experimental examination the physical and mental characteristics of men who have achieved marked success in their chosen vocations. By the application of this clinical method to men of superior attainment it is hoped that light may be thrown on the psychological foundations of their genius and, in general, on the relation between mental traits, as shown in the results of psychological tests, and actual success in life's work. This psychographic method represents the earliest methodical attempt to differentiate the various vocations from one another on the basis of special aptitudes and characteristics, as distinguished from the factor of general intelligence. Dr. E. Toulouse has already published reports of such examinations or psychographs in the cases of Zola, Dalou, and Henri Poincaré. It is the intention of this investigator to continue this line of work, utilizing from time to time such refinements of technique as may be available. As an illustration of the psychographic method, an account of the study of the eminent mathematician, Poincaré, may be given in some detail.

The investigation of Poincaré took account of such special topics as heredity, development, physical condition, sensory acuity, various kinds of memory, attention, imagery, reaction time, association of ideas, language and handwriting, character, habits and opinions. Although the tests followed a technique which the investigator recognized to have been quite imperfect and fragmentary, they are said to have yielded results quite sufficient to characterize the intellectual type of the man. The account of the tests is followed by a synthesis in which is attempted a general picture of

Poincaré's type and an interpretation of the conditions of invention and speculative genius.

From the point of view of heredity, development and general vital characteristics Poincaré was found to resemble most his mother and grandmother, who, with collateral relatives, are said to have shown special aptitude in mathematical calculation. Several male members of the family have had successful careers in neurology, law, meteorology, politics and mathematics. Poincaré's development was not precocious, although he was bright and showed, when quite young, mathematical ability of an unusual order. His history, up the age of thirty years, at which time he was elected to the Academy of Sciences, was not unlike that of many other mathematicians whose freedom from the necessity of experiment allows them to make rapid progress. He was at one time troubled with rheumatism, and in his childhood suffered from an attack of diphtheria, followed by paralysis. This attack is said to have profoundly modified his nervous system, perhaps providing the neuropathic basis for traits shown later in life, such as awkwardness, restlessness, flighty attention, distractibility and general sensori-motor deficiency.

A physical examination which dealt mainly with anthropometric measurements, strength tests, and with an inquiry into habits of eating, sleeping, and the use of narcotics, revealed nothing very unusual. Poincaré had head measurements somewhat larger than the average. He was troubled with indigestion, also with insomnia. He did not use tobacco, and indulged only sparingly in wine and coffee. He was able to work for but four hours a day, in two-hour periods, and the tendency to automatisms and the perseverance of psychic activity compelled him to cease work for some time before retiring. He disliked muscular exercise except for the automatic processes involved in walking. His absent-mindedness was a matter of common comment among his associates. The examination of his sensory and motor capacity showed Poincaré to have been rather feeble from a sensory point of view. Hearing was defective for low tones, but auditory orientation and localization were fair. He was shortsighted, but had no astigmatism; tests of the field of vision showed no abnormality. Muscular weakness of the eyes was present, which led to accommodation spasms. His general bodily movements were characterized by uncertainty, irregularity, awkwardness and hesitancy, and his muscular reflexes were prominent.

The greater number of the tests had to do with more strictly mental characteristics. Poincaré had no visual images or memories, except in the transition state between waking and sleeping, when he had frequent visual hallucinations of remarkable distinctness. In his waking life he relied chiefly on motor images and tendencies, thinking of geometrical forms in terms of optical or manual movements. He had no visual "schemes," but represented time, in his thinking, by a rotation of the eyes on their axes. In his youth he had pronounced colored hearing, which was evoked not by the form but by the sound of letters and words. He had no other synesthesias. Tests of recognition memory for length of lines, reproduction of drawings seen once, etc., are said to have shown exceptional memory capacity. The memories were held with the aid of motor imagery, and the reproduction was often not from the image but on the basis of an analysis of the material which had been presented to him. He had a memory span for digits of about eleven, as compared with the ordinary record of about eight. In the case of letters he had an auditory memory span of nine, and a visual span of seven. Mechanical memory did not seem to be particularly good, and much emphasis is laid on Poincaré's tendency to use memory devices when remembering this non-logical material; he employed analysis and incidental schemes whenever possible. He had a "remarkable facility in mental calculation," which is said not to be the rule with mathematicians. In tests of logical memory he was superior to both Zola and Dalou, and here again his memory was found to be analytical and artificial rather than mechanical. All material was arranged in a coherent scheme or system, and it was this system, rather than the material, that was remembered.

A series of cancellation and reaction-time tests showed that the simple sensory reactions were slower and more regular than those of the average person, but the motor reactions were much quicker. This accords with previous indications as to Poincaré's general motor type. The most significant thing about the reactions is said to be the wandering and unstable attention which they disclosed. It was difficult to keep Poincaré's mind on the tests, because his attention constantly wandered to the apparatus. In receiving instructions for such experiments he did not seem to comprehend what was being said, but appeared distracted and uninterested. This is the same impression he is said to have given to those whom he met in his daily relations. He was restless, could not remain in one position or stay by one task, had no patience and abandoned his work whenever it seemed to require any voluntary effort. Tests of reverie associations and of free paired associates showed absence of voluntary attention and predominance of purely verbal association tendencies. Binet's "cigarette description" test was used, and Poincaré was found to belong to Binet's first type of observer (simple description, with no evidence of reflection or judgment, no display of erudition, no expression of fancy or sentiment). His description was remarkably lucid and clear. Poincaré spoke correctly, never learned his addresses by heart, and made few corrections either in writing or in speaking. Indications of his temperament and type are said to be suggested by his handwriting.

Poincaré's opinions on various topics are given, and several peculiar habits of daily life are recorded, chiefly for the sake of emphasizing his constant air of distraction, his impatience and restlessness. He loved music; sketched a little; did not sleep soundly; and often began to work on a problem only to abandon it in the faith that it would in some way solve itself unconsciously or that the right idea would come spontaneously on some later occasion. He often began a memoir without having any conclusion in mind. He often wrote formulae automatically for the sake of the chance associations which they might bring.

These tests of Poincaré showed him to present a striking contrast to Zola, the novelist. Zola's type was found to be characterized by prominent voluntary intellectual activity, clearly conscious and intense, concentrated effort, with no tendency to perseveration of ideas after cessation of work. His thought, as disclosed by the tests, was logical, methodical, and seemed preëminently fitted for the work of mathematical deduction. His method of work was quite the opposite of that of Poincaré, who, when he met with a difficulty or with a point requiring voluntary effort, abandoned his work or proceeded to another part of it which would develop more spontaneously. The surprising thing was that a methodical, logical and persistent worker, such as Zola, should have become the prince of romance that he was. One might have expected that the mental processes of Poincaré, which were shown to be flighty, uncontrolled, spontaneous, unstable and spasmodic, would have particularly fitted him for the activity of the romancer. Instead, they found their outlet in severe mathematical and philosophical creation. Poincaré's genius is thus said to be incapable of explanation on the basis of his sensori-motor equipment, his imagination and memory, and the speed or control of his psychic activity. If his case is taken as typical, it suggests the quite unexpected result that tendency to distraction, automatisms, oscillating attention, restlessness, uncontrolled association and reliance on chance syntheses and spontaneous ideas are significant for the type of genius required in mathematics and philosophical speculation. Certainly in Poincaré's case they seem to have constituted a definite method of research.

The chief value of this examination of Poincaré does not lie in the particular results which it yielded, but in its initiation of such attempts to study in a more or less intimate and intensive way the psychological processes and type of individuals of marked achievement in special lines of work. For the purposes of vocational psychology it would be valuable to know the ways in which such admittedly superior individuals as those now being studied by Dr. Toulouse, differing as they do in their types of achievement, would react to the simple and complex tests now employed by those interested in the measurement of intelligence and special aptitudes. It is true that these psychographic methods do not yet yield results which are sufficient to inform us why the particular individuals examined were so much more successful in their work than were others who seem to have been equally favored and equally diligent. Nor have they yet revealed in any adequate way the nature or degree of the qualifications requisite for success in the vocations from which the representative men have been selected. Nevertheless the individual psychograph constitutes a suggestive method of research for the vocational psychology of the future. It represents the intensive development of the older type of "biography," based on direct observational data rather than on hearsay, conjecture and anecdote.

It is on some variation of this method that we must largely rely in our efforts to learn to what degree vocational success depends on the presence of demonstrable personal characteristics, rather than on the accidents of time, place and circumstance. It was inevitable that the first attempts to give psychographic accounts of the personality of individuals of genius should be more or less fragmentary, incomplete and experimental. This has been due partly to the rapidity with which our knowledge of mental tests has developed, and partly to the very complex and subtle types of achievement toward which these early psychographic methods have been directed. Various investigations are now under way in which these same methods are being used in the intensive examination of individuals who have engaged in simpler and more common forms of activity, with varying degrees of success. In some of these researches, for example, men who have made their life work the marketing of a specific type of commodity through direct and personal salesmanship are being submitted to intensive psychological examinations. The problem is to discover whether there is a more or less specific and recognizable type of personality which characterizes the successful salesman and differentiates him from the mediocre salesman and the utter failure. Directed toward these more familiar and more easily accessible occupations, the individual psychograph constitutes one of the most interesting forms of vocational psychology. Closely related to it, though sufficiently distinct in aim and method to merit separate presentation, is the method of the vocational psychograph, in which the work, rather than the worker, is made the object of analysis.

THE VOCATIONAL PSYCHOGRAPH

Closely related to the method of intensive examination described in the preceding section, and profitable in a somewhat different direction, is the type of psychograph represented in Professor Seashore's reports on "The Measurement of a Singer." This may be called the "vocational psychograph" as contrasted with the psychograph of the individual of genius. It proceeds by discovering first the necessary abilities and capacities which a given sort of performance demands. In the case of singing, rather more than in almost any other vocation, certain definite and fairly identifiable abilities are quite obviously required, and the degree to which they must be present for definite attainments is rather more easily discoverable.

Thus, Seashore writes: "Musical power is generally admitted to embrace certain well-recognized and fairly concrete capacities. In our commonplace judgments about ourselves and others we say: 'I have no ear for music.' 'I cannot tell a chord from a discord.' 'I cannot keep time.' 'I have no sense of rhythm.' 'I cannot tell a two-step from a waltz.' 'I cannot remember music.' 'I cannot image sounds.' 'I am not moved by music.' 'I do not enjoy music.' Or, if speaking of someone who has musical ability, we say: 'He has a deep, rich voice.' 'He never forgets an air.' 'He lives in song.' Such judgments have reference to generally admitted specific factors involved in musical capacity by virtue of a musical organization. Corresponding to these judgments of native capacity we have judgments about musical education, about musical environment, about special influences and stimuli for the development of musical talent, and about technique and success in the rendition of music. When judgments of this kind are based upon measurements, classified and adequately interpreted, they may constitute a measure of the individual as a singer.

"The measure of a singer should consist of a relatively small number of representative measurements upon specific capacities and achievements. These measurements must be set in a full survey by systematic observation and other verified information bearing upon the variation of the individual as a singer. The classification of the measurements must be based upon (1) the attributes of sound which constitute the objective aspect of music, and (2) upon fundamental and essential processes in the singer's appreciation and expression of music. From the point of view of the objective sound, we must take into account pitch (with its complexes of timbre and harmony), intensity, and duration. From the point of view of mental processes we may group the tests under the heads, sensory, motor, associational, and affective, each of these furnishing natural subdivisions."

The writer then presents an arrangement of these proposed measurements in a program, which is also recommended as the outline for a systematic description of the individual in his capacity as a singer. The sensory group of tests includes five tests under pitch, two under intensity, and one under time discrimination. The motor group includes seven tests under pitch, two under intensity, and four under time. The associational group includes two tests under imagery, three under memory, and four under ideation. The affective group contains three tests under musical appeal, and one each under reaction to musical effect and power of interpretation in singing. A copy of this program of tests is given in the Appendix.

In a chapter of his "Psychology in Daily Life,"[6] Seashore describes these special tests. He indicates their significance and suggests approximate norms for those cases for which they are at present available. For the accumulation of many of these norms, and for the conduct of the tests, special and elaborate apparatus and methods are required. For several years the workers in Seashore's laboratory have busied themselves with the problems concerned in the measurement and accumulation of norms for pitch discrimination, vividness of tone imagery, span of tone memory, consonance and dissonance, rhythmic action, intensity discrimination, voluntary control of the pitch of the voice, and the singing of intervals.

Reference to norms thus acquired shows, for example, that in the case of discrimination in voluntary control of the pitch of the voice "a record of .9 vd. means that this ability is within three per cent of the best record for individuals under similar conditions, and that those who have such control are thoroughly qualified to render a high class of music in this respect; while a record of 9 vd. falls within eight per cent of the poorest ability measured, and is characteristic of an individual who cannot sing; whereas 3 vd. represents the average ability of an untrained individual."

Again, in another connection, and with reference this time to the discrimination of tones when heard, the same investigator has suggested that one who can discriminate a difference, from a given standard pitch, of 3 vd. or less may become a musician; one whose threshold falls between 3 and 8 vd. "should have a plain musical education"; one whose discrimination is so poor that 9 to 17 vd. is the measure "should have a plain musical education only if special inclination for some kind of music is shown"; while a measure of 18 vd. or above indicates that the individual "should have nothing to do with music." These suggestions were proposed for individuals of equal age, advancement and general ability.

That is to say, there are but three persons in a hundred who, having just sung the tone which is produced by a tuning fork vibrating two hundred and fifty-six times per second, can then voluntarily and accurately change the pitch of the voice to represent the tone of a fork vibrating 256.9 times per second, a change of .9 of a vibration. But fifty persons of the hundred can produce voluntarily a change of three vibrations, and ninety-two of the hundred can produce the very large change of nine vibrations. Seashore, of course, points out that in addition to these various measurements, "there must be other measurements, statistical data, biographical information, and free observations concerning musical training, traits of temperament and attitude, spontaneous tendencies in the pursuit of music, general education and non-musical accomplishments, social circumstances and physique," and that all these in their unity must be considered in the light of expert knowledge and expert technical insight before they can be said to give an adequate estimate of the particular individual's various capacities and qualifications as a singer. Those interested in the use of psychological tests in connection with musical ability should familiarize themselves with the many original reports from Seashore's laboratory. The methods there being followed may well serve as models for future analyses of vocational demands and individual tests.

If the highly specialized work of singing calls for such complex analysis and for such varied measurements, technical skill, and arduous collection of norms and standards, one realizes the utter folly of such vocational counsel as that which vaguely recommends the candidate to "be a musician," "be a writer," etc. Indeed, we may now begin to see that it is only when each particular aspect of each particular calling is thoroughly analyzed into its elementary requirements, when reliable tests for the detection and measurement of these abilities are available, and adequate norms and standards accumulated in each case, only then can the method of the vocational psychograph come to have practical application in vocational analysis and guidance.

How far, we may now ask, has such analysis been able, as a matter of fact, to proceed with the representative types of work? So far as recorded enterprise is concerned there have been three different ways of attempting such analyses. One of these methods is that used by the various vocational bureaus in endeavoring to learn what type of individual is most in demand in the different occupations. Futile as these endeavors have been, it is nevertheless well to have them before us for our future reference and guidance. In the main the questionnaire method has been used in this connection; employers have been asked to state, in much their own way, the necessary or desirable mental and moral qualifications of those who might expect to succeed in the various kinds of work.

These replies have been collated and attempts made to secure "clinical pictures" of the type of individuals. These methods result in such characterizations as the following. The words specifying the vocation itself are omitted, and the reader is invited to guess which of the large number of possible callings is being described.

"The girl who enters —— should be able to use good language, and should dress neatly and appropriately in order to impress people agreeably. She should be able to write a legible hand, make clear figures, and spell correctly; a practical knowledge of arithmetic, especially fractions, is very important. Prime requisites for success are interest and enthusiasm and a knowledge of human nature. The born —— takes a vital interest in her ——, in her ——, and in her ——. She studies her ——, learns something of their ——, knows what their good points are, and is able to —— about them intelligently and truthfully. She is a good judge of people, and she has the sincerity and the tact which enable her to help a —— so to —— as to go away satisfied and come to her again. Such a —— is alert, energetic, and gives strongly the impression that she is in her place to —— and therefore never displays an indifferent manner toward anyone who may ask her service. Loyal to her work, she is always courteous, for loss of temper means loss of —— ——."

Now, if one but insert suitable words where the omissions occur, the paragraph remains equally applicable and illuminating when applied to any of the following occupations, diverse as they seem to be: housekeeper, waitress, stenographer, milliner, teacher, mother, doctor, nurse, cashier, sales-woman, insurance agent, bookkeeper, clinical psychologist, private secretary. The following paragraph is equally illuminating:

"If a girl wishes to succeed in —— she must be possessed with intelligence [How much?], good judgment and common sense. She must have good eyesight, good hearing and a good memory. She must have good perception and be able to concentrate her attention completely on any matter in hand. In addition to these she must be neat in executing —— work and accurate to the last degree. It is absolutely necessary that she have a good education."

It would require several trials to guess of what particular occupation this is a psychographic picture.

It is clear at once that this method yields little information of the kind we are here considering, beyond the cataloging of the general sterling virtues of mankind. The peculiar and distinctive mental functions presumably involved in the various types of work are just the ones that no one not an expert in psychological analysis could be expected adequately to portray. The so-called special qualifications, such as honesty, patience, attention, neatness, perseverance, etc., do not represent elementary psychological categories. Moreover, they are qualifications with which no legitimate sphere of human activity can afford to dispense. In the long run they are characteristics which correlate to a high degree or, indeed, perhaps help to make up and constitute what we call general intelligence. In no case is there any specification of the precise amount of these various traits that may be needed. Since the days of the faculty psychology we have ceased to think of attention, memory, will, etc., as homogeneous powers which play in a general sort of way on all sorts of material. We usually find that when an individual is inattentive to one set of facts this is largely due to his being attentively preoccupied with some other set. Still further, no tests have been proposed which satisfactorily measure such traits as honesty, perseverance, promptness. Nor is it certainly known to what degree such traits are fixed characteristics of individuals and to what degree they represent present habits and tendencies modifiable in many ways if the circumstances call for such change.

Turning from the employer himself, and his description of the ideal worker, we may inquire what happens when the professional psychologist undertakes this analysis? The only case in which an expert psychologist has attempted this is to be found in Münsterberg's recent book on "Vocation and Learning." It is there pointed out that every act and experience has its threefold aspect, the aspect of knowing, that of feeling, and that of doing. Corresponding to these three aspects, there are to be pointed out in the case of each occupation the required information, the necessary technical skill, and the special guiding personal interests and social satisfactions. In order to clarify our knowledge of the special needs of the various vocations, and presumably to aid in the guidance of individuals in their vocational choices, eleven different representative vocations are analyzed on this threefold basis. Two or three of the analyses may be given here as an indication of the results arrived at by this method at the hands of the avowed applied psychologist. The specification of the particular technical knowledge we need not include for our purpose, since this consists of information supplied through some form of education. The outline on the following page brings together the requisite abilities and the implied motives and interests, as stated for the occupations of domestic worker, architect, physician, and journalist.

Occupation	Domestic Worker	Architect	Physician	Journalist
Abilities Required	Joyful work	Esthetic sense	Social dealing	Sociability
	Energy	Imagination	Energy	Energy
	Patience	Industry	Discretion	Memory
	Teaching	Drawing	Tact	Accuracy
	Economy	Modeling	Judgment	Judgment
	Physique	Specification		Observation
		Employment of men		
	Housekeeping	Architecture	Dissection	Typewriting
	Sewing	Engineering	Microscopical Observation	Quick Expression
	Cooking	Heating	Psychotherapy	
	Nursing	Ventilating	Clinical Activity	Forceful style
	House furnishing	Construction	Surgical Technique	
Implied Personal Motives and Social Interests	Morality	Honor	Honor	Honor
	Beauty	Beauty	Truth	Truth
	Position	Position	Position	Influence
	Support	Fees	Fees	Salary
	Home Life	Comfort	Influence	Progress
	Family Welfare	Progress		
	Comfort of Community	Housing	Welfare of Community	Politics
	Family		Health	Education

	Comfort			
			Prevention of Disease	Information
				Entertainment

It is obvious that such analysis is inadequate for our purpose. For the most part the various vocations are said to be actuated by much the same motives, the leading satisfactions being honor, truth, position, beauty, progress, fees or salary, and welfare. These enumerations, of course, help us in no way to distinguish between the particular satisfactions or interests involved in the different types of work. Quite the same thing is true of the abilities required. Most of them call for energy, industry, judgment and ability to deal with people. The same might be said of prize-fighting, plumbing and peddling. And do not the journalist and the housekeeper require tact as well as the physician? Is it true that the architect alone, of the four examples here given, has use for imagination and an esthetic sense, that the domestic alone needs physical development and joyfulness? Accuracy is perhaps more necessary to success in architecture than to the pursuit of journalism, while judgment, discretion and observation would seem to be of occasional value even to the housekeeper and the architect.

In short, this type of analysis, which, whether accepted seriously or not, represents the latest word from a distinguished psychologist on the differences among the occupations, gives us no more assistance toward the basis of a vocational psychograph than did the catalogs of sterling virtues provided by the employers in their replies to the questionnaires.

Various other types of analysis have been proposed, as well as different criteria, on the basis of which the occupations might be thrown under some form of psychological classification. Thus it has been pointed out that the traditional distinctions on the basis of materials handled or type of product produced, give little indication of the type of activity involved or of the characteristics necessary for success. As Schneider has remarked: "If a boy were successful in wood-shop work, he was told he would make a good carpenter; however, wood-turning in a shop and outdoor carpentry are dissimilar types, while wood-turning in a shop and metal-turning in a shop are similar types."

Schneider has for many years considered the problems involved in adjusting human beings to congenial types of work, and prefers to classify both men and jobs on the basis of certain broad characteristics which refer more particularly to interests, habits, preferences and similar temperamental factors than to the technical psychological mechanisms employed in the work. He writes: "Every individual has certain broad characteristics and every type of work requires certain broad characteristics. The problem, then, is to state the broad characteristics, to devise a rational method to discover these characteristics (or talents) in individuals, to classify the types of jobs by the talents they require and to guide the youth with certain talents into the type of job which requires those talents. This is a big problem, but one possible of measurable solution, or, at worst, possible of a solution immeasurably superior to our present haphazard methods."

As an illustration of what Schneider means by "broad characteristics," take his distinction between the "settled" and the "roving" types. "There is a type of man who wants to get on the same car every morning, get off at the same corner, go to the same shop, ring up at the same clock, stow his lunch in the same locker, go to the same machine and do the same class of work, day after day. Another type of man would go crazy under this routine; he wants to move about, meet new people, see and do new things. The first is settled; the second is roving. The first might make a good man for a shop manufacturing a standard product; the second might make a good railroad man or a good outdoor carpenter."

Or, again, consider his distinction on the basis of "scope." "Then there are two types—one of which likes to fuss with an intricate bit of mechanism, while the other wants the task of big dimensions—the watchmaker, the engraver, the inlayer, the painter of miniatures, on the one hand; the bridge builder, the steel-mill worker, the train dispatcher, the circus man on the other. One has small scope, the other large scope."

Basing his analyses mainly on the enterprises of manufacture, construction and transportation, and recognizing that other broad characteristics would probably be listed if different types of occupation were also considered, Schneider gives a list of sixteen classifications which may be applied either to the individual or to the type of work. These are as follows:

a—Physical strength; physical weakness.
b—Mental; manual.
c—Settled; roving.
d—Indoor; outdoor.
e—Directive; dependent.
f—Original (creative); imitative.
g—Small scope; large scope.
h—Adaptable; self-centered.
i—Deliberate; impulsive.
j—Music sense.
k—Color sense.
l—Manual accuracy; manual inaccuracy.
m—Mental accuracy (logic); mental inaccuracy.
n—Concentration (mental focus); diffusion.
o—Rapid mental coördination; slow mental coördination.
p—Dynamic; static.

It must be said that the characteristics of the various types of work here enumerated are pretty much the features which have in the past guided such individuals as really chose their vocation rather than found it waiting for them, made a random selection, or seized the first available opportunity. The paired adjectives probably afford truer descriptions of various types of work than they do of types of individuals. Most individuals of one's acquaintance one would have to group neither under the one nor the other extreme, but in an average group which would show each of the opposed tendencies under special circumstances or would show no particularly marked degree of either tendency. Observation of such individuals for long periods of time and under a variety of circumstances would be required before these classifications could be made out by a stranger or by a professional counsellor. Even then such a classification could hardly be said to be psychological in any technical sense of the word, and it is not very probable that psychological training or experience would facilitate or render more reliable such classification. The question of to what degree the individual's judgment of his own characteristics may be relied on in such an analysis we must defer until a later section where that is taken up as the main subject of discussion.

The reliable vocational psychograph, which proceeds by means of a careful preliminary analysis of the qualities required in the given work, and uses specially adapted tests with reliable norms for their evaluation, is not yet available for any single occupation. The preliminary analyses so far made, whether by employer, psychologist, or engineer, give us little guidance, and until such guidance is forthcoming the special adaptation of tests and the accumulation of norms and standards cannot make much practical progress. The inadequacy of the analyses already offered should not discourage further effort in this direction. The alignment of the simple industrial processes along the general intelligence scale has already been begun. The description of the more complex tasks in terms of identifiable mental characteristics is a much more difficult task, but this very difficulty is at once a sign of the importance of the problem.

FOOTNOTES:

[6] "Conduct of Mind Series," D. Appleton & Co., New York.

CHAPTER V

SPECIALIZED VOCATIONAL TESTS AND METHODS

The absence of complete vocational psychographs has not retarded the search for tests which, though more or less fragmentary, may have vocational significance. In fact, there are some twenty types of work for which tests have already been proposed, recommended, and more or less tentatively tried out. A brief account of these, with references to the more complete literature, will be given here, and some attempt made to evaluate the tests themselves.

Substitutes for the vocational psychograph, in the way of partial and suggestive tests, have been proposed in four different forms. Since the work of the immediate future will probably develop along these same lines, these four forms will be indicated here, and typical illustrations cited in each case.

A. There is first what may be called the method of the vocational miniature. Here the entire work, or some selected and important part of it, is reproduced on a small scale by using toy apparatus or in some such way duplicating the actual situation which the worker faces when engaged at his task. Thus McComas, in testing telephone operators, constructed a miniature switchboard and put the operators through actual calls and responses, meanwhile measuring their speed and accuracy by means of chronometric attachments. Stern and others recommend tests of the fidelity of report of a witness in court by letting him observe some rehearsed scene, some motion picture representation of a series of events, or some pictorial portrayal of a scene or episode, and examining into the faithfulness with which he can describe what he there saw.

B. Closely related to this method of miniature performance is that of taking an actual piece of the work to be performed and sampling the candidate's ability by his success in this trial. Thus, in connection with the recommendation of clerks and assistants from among the boys in commercial high schools it is common to test their ability from time to time throughout their course by assigning them small pieces of work similar to that which they might later be required to perform in business offices and shops. Finding addresses and numbers in a telephone directory, carrying out involved verbal instructions and directions from memory, computing calculations, recommending action on the basis of their figures, making out a trial balance, a trial chemical analysis, etc., are common forms of this type of test. In certain cases such specimens of work have been devised in or taken into the psychological laboratory and the worker watched more closely and measured more exactly. This has been done, for instance, by Thorndike in the case of clerical workers and salesmen, by Paynter in the case of judges of trade-mark infringements, by Scott in the case of salesmen, and by others in the case of tests for handwriting experts.

C. A third method has been that of analogy. Some test is devised which bears real or supposed resemblance to the sort of situation met by the worker in the given occupational activity. The material is new, but the attitude and endeavor of the worker seem to be much the same. There is indeed usually a tacit or expressed belief that the same simple or complex mental processes or psychological functions are involved in the two cases, although the precise nature of this function has seldom been clearly stated. Thus girls employed in sorting steel ball-bearings, and also typesetters, have been selected on the basis of their speed of reaction to a sound stimulus. Münsterberg has suggested that marine officers who can quickly perceive a situation and choose an appropriate mode of reaction to it may be selected by letting candidates sort into their appropriate piles a deck of cards bearing different combinations of letters. The same investigator has described a test for motormen which, while being neither a miniature of their required work nor yet a sample of it, is said to produce in them much the same mental attitude. In another case telephone operators were tested for speed in canceling certain letters from a newspaper page, in the belief that this work involved an ability that was also required at the switchboard, although there directed to different material. McComas has described a dot-striking test for measuring accuracy of aim or motor coördination, which forms an essential factor in manipulating a switchboard.

D. Finally there are cases in which tests having vocational significance have been sought by purely haphazard and empirical ways. Thus Lough, having devised a form of substitution test in which certain characters had always to be replaced by certain others, according to a prescribed key, then proceeded to apply it to groups of commercial students. Speed of improvement was chosen as the thing of interest in respect to the test. Measures of this capacity, as shown by repeated trials with the same test day after day, were then compared with measures of ability in different types of work in which the students were engaged. It was found that the test records agreed very closely with the abilities in typewriting, fairly closely with abilities in business correspondence and stenography, whereas there was not such definite relation found between the test records and ability in learning the German language or in mathematics. The test is consequently recommended as a useful means of detecting typewriting and stenographic ability. It is not pretended that the test is a miniature of the work of such calling, nor that it is a fair sample of such work, nor even that it involves precisely the same mental functions that come into play in such work. The test records and ability in the particular type of work show high positive correlation, which means that an individual who is good or medium or poor in the one is, as a mere matter of fact, also found to be good, medium or poor in the other. Hence, without further analysis, the one may be used as the sign of the other.

Another good illustration of the use of this method is the study of Lahy, who put good, average and poor typewriters through a great number of tests of different sorts. He found that the only tests correlating closely with ability in the practical work were those for memory span, tactile and muscular sensibility, sustained attention, and equality of strength in the two hands.

Perhaps the most perfect example of this purely empirical procedure is the investigation which has now been conducted for several years by Mrs. Woolley and her co-workers in Cincinnati. Children who leave the grades to enter directly into some sort of industrial occupation are examined by a miscellaneous assortment of simple mental tests. These records are preserved, and the subsequent successes or failures of the pupils in the various sorts of work undertaken by them in later life are as carefully recorded as is possible. It is hoped that when a sufficient amount of material of this nature has been accumulated the two sets of data may be compared and information thereby secured concerning the relation between ability in the tests and the types and degrees of industrial fitness. At present only the test records have been published.

In a recent investigation an attempt was made to discover, by this empirical method, a set of mental tests which would aid in the selection of efficient workers in a specific field. Thirty workers who were already employed under fairly comparable conditions of work were taken as subjects in a preliminary search for tests of value. These thirty people were each put through a series of "association tests," of the familiar laboratory form, naming opposites, naming colors and forms, completing mutilated passages, following hard directions, giving responses bearing specified relations to stimulus words, cancellation and number checking, etc. While these tests were in progress, during a period of several days, the thirty workers were rated by three supervisors who were familiar with their work at the actual task, and who had for some time been observing their performance with a view to making subsequent judgments. Each supervisor arranged the thirty workers in an order of merit, according to his or her impression of their relative efficiency. The judgments of these three supervisors were then averaged and each worker assigned a final position on the basis of these averages. This was believed to be as accurate a measure of actual ability as could be secured under the complex conditions of work.

The results of these ratings were then compared with the results of the mental tests. Some of the tests were found not to correlate with the ratings for actual working efficiency. Three tests showed definite and positive correlations, as follows: *Color-Naming* (thirty-seven per cent), *Hard Directions* (forty per cent), *Completion* (thirty-three per cent). When results from these three tests were combined, the records correlated with the ratings by a coefficient of fifty-five per cent. These three tests were then accepted as having value in the selection of good operators, and search was continued for further tests which might also yield positive correlations. This investigation is again an illustration of the purely empirical method.

These four procedures in the search for useful vocational tests, in the absence of complete vocational psychographs, are quite generally recognized to be but tentative expedients of an explorative character. Individual workers have not always clearly recognized the principles involved in their work, but have proceeded as best they could under the special circumstances. Each method has its own defects and advantages. The miniature model has the advantage of concreteness and apparent relevance, but, as Münsterberg points out, "a reduced copy of an external apparatus may arouse ideas, feelings and volitions which have little in common with the processes of actual life." This writer is inclined to believe, on the basis of his experiments so far, that "experiments with small models of the actual industrial mechanism are hardly appropriate for investigations in the field of economic psychology. The essential point for the psychological experiment is not the external similarity of the apparatus, but exclusively the inner similarity of the mental attitude. The more the external mechanism with which or on which the action is carried out becomes schematized, the more the action itself will appear in its true character."

The second method we have described, viz., that of using as the test a real sample of the work done, has certain very obvious advantages. On the other hand, for the vocational test of this type to be at all significant, either the sort of work involved in the occupation must be fairly uniform and homogeneous in all its different circumstances (as in the case of typewriting at dictation, or in the work of filing clerks, accountants, etc.), or else there must be included a large number of samples representing all the various unrelated sorts of work. Moreover, in neither case is the test in any peculiar sense psychological. Such tests could perhaps be best conducted by the employer himself. In fact, employment on trial, which is a common method of selecting operatives and assistants, is a time-honored form of this test, which is not necessarily improved either by calling it psychological or by putting it in charge of a general expert or by removing it to the laboratory.

The third form of procedure is full of all sorts of difficulties and sources of error, many of which are, at the present stage of our knowledge, irremediable. In selecting a new test which will involve the same mental attitude and call for the exercise of the same psychological functions as are needed in the work itself, we are handicapped by the unreliability of the introspection of the examinee and also by our inadequate ability to recognize, identify and classify psychological functions even when we are confident that these are present. The statement of motormen that the manipulation of a crank in connection with a strip of checkered paper makes them feel quite as they do when guiding their cars through a crowded thoroughfare is far from a guaranty "that the mental function which they were going through had the greatest possible similarity with their experience on the front platform of the electric car." It is much more conceivable that the "mental attitude" referred to was merely the vague feeling that "Something is happening now," "This keeps me busy," or "What a nuisance this thing is." And even if we knew the mental functions involved, as would be demanded by the vocational psychograph method, we are still a long way from the time when we can exhibit even a single psychological test and state just what function or functions its performance does or does not, may or may not, involve. Indeed we do not even know what the various distinct mental functions are, or whether, as a matter of fact, there are such distinct functions.

After all, the miscellaneous, random, and purely empirical method of Lough, Lahy and Woolley seems to be the most promising experimental procedure for the immediate present, and perhaps for some time to come. This method is, to be sure, but a rough, provisional and unanalyzed expedient. It calls for long and patient coöperative labor. It does not at once afford us the systematic scientific insight which we may wish we possessed. But it will at least save us from the delusion that we already possess such insight, and it should serve to check the fervent and semi-religious zeal that leads us to mistake prophecy for service. Analysis and classification of the results which this method yields are possible when the results are accumulated in adequate measure.

It is essential that interest in this eminently practical use of the psychological laboratory be sustained among those who are responsible for the further promotion of its methods and problems. But it is undesirable that public expectation should be strenuously directed toward the laboratory until it has done more than the outlining of a series of problems and the initiation of preliminary efforts toward their solution. These specialized vocational methods, the miniature, the sampling, the analogy, and the empirical procedure, constitute four definite and promising instruments of research. They have yielded results of such demonstrable practical value, in the selection of special types of workers and in the detection of particular aptitudes and abilities, that the application of selected mental tests has already come to play an important rôle in the placement and training departments of a considerable number of industrial and commercial concerns. While the more slowly developing individual and vocational psychographs are being perfected, these specialized vocational tests will not only serve the purposes of temporary assistance and expedience, but the results derived from their intelligent use and their further patient elaboration will contribute materially toward the establishment of more complete and systematic technique.[7]

CHAPTER VI

SELF-ANALYSIS AND THE JUDGMENT OF ASSOCIATES

THE SELF-ANALYSIS OF THE INDIVIDUAL

We have now reviewed the vocational efforts of primitive magic, medieval clairvoyance, phrenology, physiognomics, industrial education, the vocational survey, the individual psychograph of genius, the vocational psychograph, the graded scales of intelligence tests, and the four proposed types of specialized vocational tests.

We have yet to consider three further methods available for the purposes of vocational psychology, that of "self-analysis," and that of the "consensus of opinion" of one's associates, and that of inferring the characteristics of the individual from his achievement in the work of the school curriculum. In the absence of more reliable ways of determining the capacities, interests and vocational aptitudes of individuals in the past, and whenever there was any question of selection, fitness, or choice, four vague methods have often been followed. (1) Either the individual undertook the first available type of employment, tried it out, and then persevered in it or abandoned it for a trial at some other type of work until a suitable occupation was found; or (2) he continued at the original work and made the most of the results and of the ensuing satisfactions or dissatisfactions; or (3) he felt more or less clearly drawn to some particular occupation because of a keen interest in it or because he believed himself to be particularly likely to succeed in it because of his own analysis of his aptitudes and characteristics; or (4) he consulted friends and associates, asking them to advise him on the basis of their impression of his individuality and powers.

The unsatisfactoriness, waste and misery of the first two of these methods are largely responsible for the development of a conscious attempt at the vocational guidance of youth. Perhaps if more use were made of the two remaining methods we should never have been moved to initiate the laborious work called for by the psychographic and the test methods. Not enough critical attention has been given to the methods of self-analysis and to the validity of the judgments passed on us by our associates. The difficulty encountered when one seeks for information on such questions as the following indicates the desirability of further and closer study of these matters.

1. In the individual's analysis of his own personality, are formal guidance and method needed, is special terminology useful, and the recorded experience of others an aid?

2. If so, what sort of guide or scheme or system may such self-analysis profitably follow?

3. Have such guides to the introspective analysis of the self been formulated, and by whom, where, and when?

4. How reliable and consistent are an individual's judgments of his own characteristics, interests, and aptitudes? Has one any constant tendency to overestimate or underestimate himself?

5. Do the degree of reliability and consistency, and this constant error vary in any way with the individual, with the circumstances, and with the particular trait that is being estimated?

6. How is the individual's judgment of himself likely to compare with the impression of him which his associates form? To what degree does this vary with the individual, the trait, and the associates?

7. What relation exists between the individual's opinion of himself and the results of objective measurements of him, such as those afforded by psychological tests? How do the results of tests compare with the judgments of associates?

8. Are individuals who themselves possess a given trait in high degree better judges of that trait in themselves or in others than are those who possess the trait in less degree?

9. What intercorrelations exist between the estimates of self and others, when different traits are compared?

10. In the case of people in school, what relations exist between the self-estimate, the estimate of others, and the results of tests, on the one hand, and school standing, academic success, and extra-academic activities? What relation between these factors and successfulness in later life?

On the first three of these questions I shall indicate in following sections such material as is available, pointing out where the more valuable and detailed information may be found. On the remaining seven questions recorded information is much rarer. Here I shall summarize the available material and shall also present tentative answers based on an original investigation which was conducted for the express purpose of calling more definite attention to the problems, as well as to suggest fruitful methods, and at least make a beginning in the accumulation of facts concerning these very interesting features of human nature.

There is perhaps no proof required that complete and systematic self-analysis is more desirable than random and undirected introspections, whatever value may be attached to the results of such analysis. Whatever be the purpose of self analysis, it will be the more useful and suggestive the more completely it compasses the total range of capacities and inclinations. Comparison of different analyses by different individuals should result in a synthesis of traits, an acceptable terminology and a mode of statement better calculated to throw light on individual equipment than is secured by the methods of casual and unguided rumination. So far as possible such analyses should proceed in terms of identifiable, comparable and measurable characteristics rather than by the vague categories of conversation and literary description. Such categories, traits and terminology should be used as will best enable the individual not only to state his own reactions in figures of speech, but also to compare himself with his immediate associates and with characters less directly known.

One of the first attempts to draw up a list of fundamental qualities as an aid in the inventory of a given individual's particular nature was made by Professor Cattell in an article concerning the characteristics of men of science. Twenty-four traits are enumerated, as follows:

Physical Health Reasonableness
Mental Balance Clearness

Intellect	Independence
Emotions	Coöperativeness
Will	Unselfishness
Quickness	Kindliness
Intensity	Cheerfulness
Breadth	Refinement
Energy	Integrity
Judgment	Courage
Originality	Efficiency
Perseverance	Leadership

Of this list Thorndike has written: "These elements of manhood or components in mental structure hail from a mixture of psychological theory and general reflection on human behavior. It is regrettable that the list has not been published more widely and used in a variety of connections. It seems probable that these significant nouns may in many cases be paralleled by natural units of mental organization-atoms in the human compound. I venture to suggest also, as at least a provisional principle of organization, the instincts or original tendencies of man as a species, it being my opinion that some of the terms of the above list refer to rather complex concatenations of traits in man's nature which have only the artificial unity of producing some defined result in human life."

Partridge, in his "Outline of Individual Study," gives an account of methods whereby the teacher may assist the young child in discovering his or her particular physical and mental constitution. The book contains a brief outline for such study and enumerates many pages of words descriptive of human nature. The main aspects of the mental life of children are taken up in successive chapters and discussed in a general way, with suggestions in the way of tests, problems, questions, points of observation, etc.

The "Family History Book" (Bulletin No. 7) of the Eugenics Record Office contains a scheme, arranged by Drs. Hoch and Amsden, for the examination of the personality of persons suspected of mental abnormality. This scheme is further elaborated by Wells in an outline to be referred to at a later point in this chapter. In the "Trait Book" (Bulletin No. 6) of this same office there is to be found a long list of traits descriptive of human beings, including physical and physiological as well as nervous and mental characteristics. These traits are classified for convenient reference and record according to a decimal key. The pamphlet also contains classified lists of diseases, crimes, and occupations. Various other bulletins issued by the Eugenics Record Office will also be found both interesting and suggestive to those interested in the study of self-analysis, heredity and individual differences. They contain nothing, however, of immediate vocational applicability.

Dr. F. L. Wells has made a comparative study and synthesis of the schemes proposed by Cattell, Hoch and Amsden, Heymans and Wiersma, and Davenport, supplementing these at certain points and suggesting a method of giving more or less quantitative form to the characterizations. It is obvious that an outline of this sort can be used in expressing the personality of another individual as well as for the purposes of self-analysis. Such an outline is of value not only for general knowledge or for vocational study but also in the examination into questions of mental health, pathological tendencies and trends, predispositions leading to or favoring mental instability, etc. Wells describes fourteen phases or aspects of human personality, and under each phase presents guiding questions, suggestive clues, and sub-features. Especially convenient and helpful is the method of giving an approximate quantitative statement which facilitates comparison and summation. Suitable marks assigned to the several different characteristics under each of the fourteen main headings (there are in all about ninety-five subtraits) serve to indicate marked, distinct or doubtful presence, or marked, distinct or doubtful deficiency or aversion.

The main headings given by Wells are as follows:

1. Intellectual Processes (5 subtopics)
2. Output of Energy (4 subtopics)
3. Self Assertion (7 subtopics)
4. Adaptability (5 subtopics)
5. General Habits of Work (5 subtopics)
6. Moral Sphere (6 subtopics)
7. Recreative Activities (16 subtopics)
8. General Cast of Mood (3 subtopics)
9. Attitude Toward Self (4 subtopics)

10. Attitude Toward Others (7 subtopics)
11. Reactions to Attitude Toward Self and Others (12
    subtopics)
12. Position Towards Reality (5 subtopics)
13. Sexual Sphere (9 subtopics)
14. Balancing Factors (6 subtopics)

The complete outline, accompanied by much suggestive discussion and comment on the constitution, development and types of human personality, is published in the issue of the *Psychological Review* for July, 1914. It should be carefully read by all interested in this type of individual analysis.

One of the most carefully planned, easily available and concretely serviceable outlines for self-analysis is that recently formulated and published by Yerkes and LaRue under the title "Outline of a Study of the Self" (Harvard University Press, 1914). The authors of this outline have found that a study of ancestry, development and present constitution is an extremely profitable task. They present this guide as an aid to such systematic and thorough study. The purpose of such study is threefold: (1) to help the individual understand himself or herself; (2) to help the individual understand and sympathize with others; (3) to arouse interest in the study of heredity, environmental influences, eugenics and euthenics.

The "Outline" is put together on the looseleaf system, with blank pages for records and replies. Under the heading "Ancestral History of the Self" are given the "Record of Family Traits" of the Eugenics Record Office, and many supplementary questions concerning physical, mental, moral and social traits of near relatives, with suggestions as to their classification and evaluation. Under "Development or Growth of the Self" and "The Self of Today" the prenatal, infantile, childhood and adolescent periods and the present time are each provided with questions concerning characteristics, influences, growth, temperament, inclinations, habits, capacities and social relations. Under "The Significance of the Characteristics of the Self" are given questions concerning vocational demands, equipment, and ambitions; marital propensities and fitness; responsibilities and preparation for parenthood; and the "Index to the Germ Plasm" of the Eugenics Record Office is considered. A final section invites reflection on "The Duties of the Self as a Member of Social Groups" in the light of physical and mental constitution, moral and religious tendencies, vocational abilities, and marital and parental relations and duties.

Such attempts to present suggestive outlines for self-analysis or for the inventory of the traits of others are both commendable and timely. That they are but beginnings in the right direction their authors commonly recognize. Their supporting idea is not that employers, teachers or physicians should take the individual's replies to these questions as embodying information which the individual did not previously know about himself. The individual, in attempting to express and analyze his inclinations and reactions, may find them clarified and ordered in the process. He is likely to discover at a very early point in his record how little he is really able to say about himself with assurance. If this should induce a humility which would lead him to more careful self-scrutiny, such value as this subjective stock-taking may have will surely tend to be enhanced.

THE JUDGMENT OF ASSOCIATES

No less important than the correct evaluation of the individual's self-analysis is the problem of evaluating the judgments which his acquaintances pass on his mental constitution and qualifications. Not only does the youth often determine his choice of a vocation by relying on the advice of his associates, teachers, and friends, but his success in securing an opportunity to undertake any kind of work whatsoever often depends on the oral or written estimate of some other person of whom inquiry is made. Selection on the basis of the testimonial and the recommendation has come to be a traditional vocational step.

"The problem of judgment of character is one which is continually confronting people of all classes and stations. In many instances the correct estimate of a person's character is of vital importance. The success of officers of administration from the President of the United States to the school superintendent of a small village depends often on their ability to choose for their subordinates persons of the proper character. In everyday life one's happy choice of friends, one's ability to sell goods, to persuade people to accept a new point of view or doctrine, to get on harmoniously with people in general in all the various occupations of life, depend upon one's ability to estimate the powers, capacities, and characteristics of people. To those who have to make personal recommendations or to make use of those made by others, this question of judgment of character is a grave one. Is it possible for one to judge at all fairly the character of another?"[8]

We are concerned here not with inference from physiognomic features and anthropometric measurements, but with impressions based on the observed conduct, expression and achievement of the individual who is in question, his or her characteristic behavior, attitudes, activities, reactions, and accomplishments. When the individual being judged is a total stranger and the judgment is immediate, estimates of character are of course merely of the type discussed in preceding sections on phrenology and physiognomy.

Professor Cattell once requested twelve acquaintances of five scientific men to grade these five men in the various traits of character to which we have referred on page 127. The grades assigned were to represent the position of the individual in his group. Thus a grade of twenty-five per cent would mean that the individual belonged in the lowest one-quarter of the total group of scientific men in the country, in the trait so marked, three-fourths of the group being superior to him in this trait. A grade of one hundred per cent would mean that the individual so graded would belong among the highest one per cent of all the scientific men in the country, in the trait so marked. When these records were compiled it was seen that in the case of certain traits, such as energy, perseverance, efficiency, the twelve judges differed much less among themselves than when judging other traits, such as cheerfulness, kindliness, unselfishness. It is interesting to note that the traits on which the judges agreed closely represent the individual's reactions to objective things, whereas the traits on which they disagreed most represent the individual's reactions toward other people.

There are, of course, several reasons for this result. In the first place the reactions of an individual to objects, as displayed in his daily work, are matters of common knowledge and are likely to leave objective and even measurable evidence such as wealth, books, buildings, etc. Reactions to other individuals are more likely to vary with the occasion and with the companion, and are also likely to be deliberately controlled, inhibited or assumed, in the interest of more objective and remote ends. This would mean that whereas in the first case all the judges were dealing with much the same material, in the form of actual products of the traits in question, in the second case they were more or less likely to have in mind rather different reactions or occasions of a more strictly personal character.

The problem of the validity of judgments of the various traits was considered in a more detailed way by Norsworthy, from whose account of her inquiry we have already quoted. She chose the traits enumerated by Cattell, and performed several experiments to determine the reliability of judgments of this sort. Thus she had five intimate acquaintances independently grade a sixth person for her possession of these twenty-four traits, on two different occasions several weeks apart.

Two things were clearly shown. In the first place the individual judges, in their second trials, did not diverge far from their first ratings. In the second place the double judgments of the five different judges did not diverge far from each other. These two facts "prove that the ratings do stand for some actual quantitative value and are not subject to mere chance. The validity of the judgments, in the sense of their correspondence with the actual character of X is then only a matter of the impartiality of the group of judges."

Similar results were found in the judgments of nine members of a college society by five of their comrades, and in the judgments of a teacher by two hundred college students. It was apparent also that judges differ from one another in the general accuracy of their gradings. Some of them agree closely with the consensus of opinion, while others depart, in varying degrees, from the average or correct estimate. It was also seen that, in estimating certain individuals, judges with presumably equal acquaintance with those being judged agreed closely with one another. Other persons had produced quite different impressions on the different judges and this was revealed in the greater divergence of the grades assigned to such persons.

As in the case of Cattell's results, figures are presented showing the degree of divergence among the judges in estimating the different traits. In the table on page 139 these figures are given, as shown in the records of five judges in one of Norsworthy's experiments, and the records of the twelve judges in Cattell's investigation. The average variability or degree of divergence for all the twenty-four traits is taken as the standard and each trait compared with this standard. A variability of one hundred thus indicates the average amount of disagreement. Figures smaller than one hundred indicate that the agreement was closer than average, and figures larger than one hundred indicate that here the judges disagreed by more than the average amount.

Naturally, there is not perfect agreement in these two cases, since the one set of data is from a group of girls judging one another on the basis of their acquaintance as social comrades and fellow students, while the other set is from scientific men judging one another on the basis of less constant association and largely on acquaintance in lecturing, research, teaching and the writing of articles and books. Moreover, results from groups of only five judges in the one case and only twelve in the other are subject to considerable variable error. In spite of these facts, interesting suggestions are afforded by the comparison.

TABLE 1

VARIABILITY IN JUDGING DIFFERENT TRAITS

Trait	Relative Divergence of Different Judges		
	Cattell, 12 Judges	Norsworthy, 5 Judges	Average of Both Experiments
Efficiency	75.0	92.4	83.7 (Close
Originality	95.2	77.2	86.2 Agreement)
Quickness	90.0	88.0	89.0
Intellect	95.2	92.0	93.6
Perseverance	75.0	101.0	88.1
Judgment	100.0	78.7	89.4 (Fair
Will	85.1	98.1	91.8 Agreement)
Breadth	100.0	92.4	96.2
Leadership	90.0	102.9	96.5

Clearness	104.9	75.7	90.3
Mental Balance	110.2	81.8	96.0
Intensity	85.1	113.7	99.4
Reasonableness	115.0	86.4	100.7 (Slight
Independence	104.9	98.5	101.7 Agreement)
Refinement	90.0	116.5	103.5
Physical Health	115.0	92.4	103.7
Emotions	120.0	91.0	105.5
Energy	75.0	109.0	91.0
Courage	100.0	119.5	109.8
Unselfishness	115.0	106.0	110.5 (Little
Integrity	104.9	130.1	117.5 Agreement)
Coöperativeness	125.0	113.5	119.3
Cheerfulness	130.0	112.0	121.0
Kindliness	120.0	125.7	122.9

It is to be noted that certain traits show small divergence in both cases. Thus intellect, quickness, originality and efficiency have low measures of variability, both for the sorority members and for the men of science. The average percentages of these four traits are, in the order named, 93.6, 89.0, 86.2, and 83.7. These, it is to be observed, are the traits which are likely to yield objective products. The more personal, social and moral traits, however, such as coöperativeness, unselfishness, kindliness, cheerfulness, and integrity, show large divergence of the individual judgment with both groups. The average measures of variability for these traits, in the order named, are 119.3, 110.5, 122.9, 121.0, and 117.5. There is another group of traits which, while showing only about average variability with one group, show close agreement in the other: such as will, judgment, perseverance, leadership and breadth. These, it is clear, are more nearly like the objective than they are like the personal traits. Then there are several traits which, while showing only average variability with one group, show large divergences in the other, such as courage and independence. These would seem to be more nearly like the more strictly personal traits.

Norsworthy points out that the traits about which inquiries are commonly made in recommendation blanks sent out by teachers' agencies, employment bureaus, and employers, tend to be those on which, according to her results, individual opinion is least reliable. Traits such as originality, judgment, clearness and quickness, on which judgments are most unanimous and consistent, are usually omitted from these blanks. This indicates the desirability of a more careful examination into the general validity of this type of judgment.

Here, then, as in all the other topics that we have had occasion to discuss, we find that our present knowledge is far from adequate to meet the demands of practical life. Available results are tentative only, but they are so suggestive as to afford a series of interesting problems for further investigation. The validity of judgments of associates varies with the judge, with the trait in question, and with the person who is being estimated. But it does not vary at random; it varies in what seem to be fairly definite, common, and determinable ways. That we do not know more about the precise nature of these variations means merely that few persons have taken the trouble to inquire into the matter.

The use of oral and written recommendations, testimonials, "characters," and letters of introduction should be based on a careful study of these materials. Especially should we know more than we now do concerning the reliability of judgment in the case of the different traits, the likelihood that the verdict of a single judge will agree with the consensus of opinion, the relation of these judgments to the individual's self-estimate, and the accordance of both these with the results of objective performance. In the following chapter some of these questions will be further considered.

FOOTNOTES:

[8] Norsworthy, "The Validity of Judgments of Character," in "Essays in Honor of William James," p. 553.

CHAPTER VII

EXPERIMENTAL STUDY OF SELF-ANALYSIS, ESTIMATES OF ASSOCIATES AND THE RESULTS OF TESTS

As we have already remarked, it would be of scientific interest and of practical value in vocational psychology if we knew something more or less precise concerning the reliability of the individual's self-analysis. It would be of equal interest and value to know in what ways the results of such introspection compare with the judgments of friends and the results of actual measurement. By way of initiating investigations of these and related questions the following experiments have been carried out. The results to be reported are so suggestive as to make very desirable a continuation and extension of researches of this kind.

From a list of about one hundred and fifty students in their third college year each member of the group was asked to indicate by marking, as 3, 2, 1, or 0, the degree of her acquaintance with each of the others. From the total list a group of twenty-five were selected, all of whom were acquainted with one another. At intervals varying from two weeks to a month each individual was given twenty-five slips of paper bearing the names of these acquaintances and including the individual's own name. She was asked to arrange the members of the group in order of merit, on each occasion, according to their degree of possession of some one trait, such as neatness, humor, intelligence, conceit, etc. Thus in the case of neatness, for example, the twenty-five persons were to be placed in a series with the neatest at one end, the most slovenly at the other end, and all the others arranged in their appropriate intermediate positions, as based on the judge's personal opinion of them. The judge was to include her own name in the series, placing herself where she believed herself to belong in relation to her twenty-four acquaintances. The record was then handed in, in an apparently anonymous way, but, unknown to the individuals, accurate record was kept, identifying each arrangement. This was done in order that the judges might be encouraged to the greatest degree of frankness both in judging their acquaintances and in recording their self-estimates. The different arrangements were separated by considerable intervals of time, so that the judgments of the various traits should be influenced as little as possible by the memory of where the different individuals in the list had been placed for other traits on previous occasions.

In addition to this part of the experiment, each person was put through a series of seven psychological tests, all of which had been rather generally found to give results which revealed, to a very high degree of correctness, the general intelligence of people when this was determined in other ways, as by mental age, school grade, academic marks, opinions of teachers, judgments of friends, etc. The particular tests used were the Graded Completion Test, described in a previous section, and six so-called Association Tests, recommended by the Committee on Standardization of Tests of the American Psychological Association. They are usually known as Directions Test, Opposites Test, Supraordinate Concept Test, Whole-Part Test, Action-Agent Test, and Mixed Relations Test. Copies of the forms used in these tests are given in the Appendix.

All of these tests involve the demand for the quick and accurate perception of and reaction to the relations of things or ideas to each other. Everything indicates that this ability is most important and determining in the composition of that characteristic which we vaguely call "general intelligence," especially if we are dealing with people with school experience.

Furthermore, the academic marks of scholarship assigned to these twenty-five students by their instructors in different college branches during three terms of college work were secured from the official records. Judgments of the degree to which the different students had been prominent in extra-academic activities during their college career were made by officers of the college who had known them during this time. Photographs of the twenty-five persons, of the same general style and size, were secured also, as well as characteristic specimens of their handwriting.

This experiment having been completed, a similar investigation was undertaken with twenty-five members of the senior class. The same method of procedure was followed as in the first case, the same traits judged, the same tests administered, etc. This second investigation thus affords a check on the results of the first study. When the results from the two investigations are averaged we have figures of considerable reliability, and fairly accurate data on numerous interesting questions.

Probably never before have such diverse ways been employed in attempting to get intensive measurements of the individuality. The material enables us to throw preliminary and suggestive light on many of the questions we have already raised. It should of course be fully recognized that the results of this little investigation cannot be generalized into final conclusions which will be true in other cases, without further verification of them. The results show only what happened in this case, and only to that degree do they suggest what we may expect to be generally true. Many similar studies must be made, under all sorts of conditions and by a variety of methods, before we shall have the final answers to our questions. But the results are no less valuable because of their lack of finality. Tentative as they may be, they nevertheless show what happened in the only recorded attempt to find answers to the questions we have been considering. If the reader will now turn back to page 124 he will note how numerous, important, and complex these questions are, and how little is at present known about them.

Turning now to our experiment, it will be observed that only in the case of intelligence do we have what purport to be objective measures of a trait, viz., the results of the psychological tests and the academic records. But we have, in the average of the judgments of the twenty-five individuals, in the case of this and also of the various other traits, what constitutes as valid a measurement as it is possible to secure under the circumstances. Neatness, conceit, humor, beauty, etc., are not to be conceived as substances of which the different individuals possess different amounts. These traits are mainly ways of behaving or ways of impressing our neighbors. No better measure of them exists than the actual statement of what this impression is. Just as the value of a commodity depends entirely on what, as a matter of fact, people can be persuaded to pay for it, so the beauty, conceit, neatness, etc., of an individual are mainly constituted by the kind of impression the individual makes on those about him. At least we may be sure that only to the degree that such traits actually manifest themselves and thus determine the reactions of others toward the individual concerned, only to that degree do the traits have vocational significance. Lovableness is just the degree to which people actually have affection for us; eminence is just the degree to which the individual becomes approvingly known; and kindliness and benevolence are present to just the degree that people are actually gratified and comforted by our conduct.

Let us turn at once to the actual results of our experiments. It will perhaps be best to ask specific questions about them and in the case of each question present the data and draw such conclusions as the figures warrant. In the figures which follow I have averaged together the results from the two investigations, so that our conclusions or suggestions may have the highest possible validity. In some other connection it would be interesting to compare the two sets of data, and to attempt to explain certain differences which are to be found between them. But in the present instance it is our chief concern to exhibit the method of procedure and to indicate the type of information which may be secured from such investigations. Many more such studies must be made before the results can be said to apply to human nature at large, or before the tendencies discovered can legitimately be expected to be present in the case of any particular individual.

I. How do the self-estimates of these fifty persons agree with the judgments passed on them by their acquaintances? The following table gives, in the case of each of the nine traits studied, the average deviation of the self-estimates of the various individuals from the median position assigned them by their twenty-four associates, and also the average deviation[9] among these twenty-four associates in their judgments of each individual. The figure given is in terms of the number of positions in the total scale of twenty-five possible positions. Thus, in the case of neatness, the figures mean that, whereas each individual, in the long run, displaces herself by 5.8 positions from her true or median position, the twenty-four associates deviate on the average by only 4.5 places in their judgments of another person. That is to say, the individual's error in judging herself is somewhat greater than the average error of her friends in their judgments of her. The individual does not judge herself as accurately as she is judged by her friends.

TABLE 2

Error of Self-estimates Compared with Error of Judgments of 24 Associates

	A. D. of Assoc.	A. E. of Self-Est.
Neatness	4.5	5.8
Intelligence	3.7	6.0
Humor	4.5	7.3
Conceit	4.1	5.7
Beauty	3.8	6.0
Vulgarity	3.5	6.1
Snobbishness	4.8	5.1
Refinement	5.9	7.2
Sociability	4.7	5.4

In all cases the individual places herself farther from her true position than do her friends on the average. The average of all the deviations of associates is 4.4 places; that of all the individual self-estimates is 6.1 places. That is to say, in general the error of self-estimation tends to be half again as great as the average error of the judgments of associates. In other words, these students do not judge themselves as accurately as their friends judge them, if the average position assigned the individual by the group of twenty-four associates may be taken as a fair measure of the individual's true status in the group.

II. Is there any constant tendency toward overestimation or underestimation, in the case of the individual's self-estimates, and if so, how does this tendency vary with the trait in question? It may be said in answer to this question, first, that in the case of none of the traits do all the individuals consistently either overrate or underrate themselves. But if the self-displacements be averaged algebraically, certain very definite tendencies toward constant errors are revealed. The following table shows the constant error in the case of each trait. In the case of "undesirable" traits (conceit, vulgarity and snobbishness) this constant error is toward underestimation. On the average, these individuals rank themselves as less conceited, less vulgar and less snobbish than they really are, as judged by the combined opinion of their associates. In the case of all the remaining traits (the "desirable" ones) the general tendency is toward overestimation. The amount or degree of this overestimation varies considerably from trait to trait. It is greatest in the cases of refinement and humor, in which traits there are constant errors of +6.3 and +5.2 places. In the cases of neatness, intelligence, and sociability the overestimation is only about half as large as in these two traits, while in the case of beauty there is really no constant error.

TABLE 3

SHOWING CONSTANT TENDENCIES TOWARD OVERESTIMATION (+) AND UNDERESTIMATION (-) OF SELF

Trait	Constant Error	Number Overestimating Themselves	Number Underestimating Themselves
Refinement	+6.3	40	10
Humor	+5.2	39	11
Intelligence	+3.0	34	16
Sociability	+2.2	34	16
Neatness	+1.8	25	25
Beauty	+0.2	25	25
Conceit	-1.7	24	26
Snobbishness	-2.0	18	32
Vulgarity	-4.2	17	33

Another way of expressing these constant tendencies is to give in each case the number of people in the group of fifty observers who tend in each direction. These figures are given in the last two columns of the above table. It is clear at once that in the case of the first four traits the tendency is predominantly in the direction of overestimation; in the next three traits the two tendencies are evenly balanced, while in the last two the general tendency is strongly toward underestimation.

It is of course difficult to say, in this connection, just how accurately the figures given portray the real self-estimation of the different individuals, and to what degree they indicate merely what the individual will do with her own name in the case of such an experiment. Natural modesty might easily lead one to place her own name lower in the scale for a given trait than she really believed herself to belong. If this were the case, we might then infer that the figures we have presented, although qualitatively suggestive, were not quantitatively reliable. They would, in other words, express smaller degrees of overestimation and underestimation than were really present in the consciousness of our observers. Here, as in all the results of this investigation, the figures are given only as indicating what individuals actually do when asked to rank themselves among their associates. Our conclusion on this point is that they tend to overestimate or to underestimate themselves, according to the "desirableness" or "undesirableness" of the trait in question. Individual differences in these tendencies are everywhere apparent. Thus, in neatness, individuals S and H stand about equally high (S being ninth and H being thirteenth), but S underestimates herself by thirteen places, while H overestimates herself by ten places.

In a third experiment of this same kind another group of twenty-five college seniors, in the same school and during the preceding year, had judged each other, including themselves, for the traits, efficiency, energy, kindliness and originality. The data from this experiment are not given here in full, since the method was precisely that of the two investigations we have just described, and since all of the results must be held as only suggestive of what may be expected to happen in the long run. These seniors also showed a general tendency to rate themselves somewhat higher than they were rated by their associates. The amount of overestimation varied with the trait, all the traits in this case being of the "desirable" sort. Since the conditions of this third experiment were quite the same as those of the investigation just described in greater detail, except that a different group of individuals were concerned, it is perhaps fair to treat the results as comparable, and to include the measures of constant error along with the preceding records. The results from all the groups are included in the following table, which shows the constant tendency in the case of thirteen traits.

Trait	Constant Error	Trait	Constant Error
Refinement	+6.3	Neatness	+1.8
Humor	+5.2	Originality	+1.2
Kindliness	+4.0	Beauty	+0.2
Energy	+3.8	Conceit	-1.7
Intelligence	+3.0	Snobbishness	-2.0
Sociability	+2.2	Vulgarity	-4.2
Efficiency	+2.1		

Data from certain other investigations also tell us something about these tendencies in judging ourselves and others. Thus, in an investigation by the writer,[10] a number of persons were set to work at the continuous performance of a series of mental and physical tests. After each trial the performer was required to judge whether he had done better or worse than usual on this occasion. In each case another person was required to watch the performer, and to judge, in the capacity of witness, whether the performance had been better or worse than usual for the individual who was doing the work.

The data showed that although an observer is no more "sensitive" to gain in efficiency than he is to loss, he is predisposed to judge both himself and another performer whom he is watching as having done "better than usual" rather than "worse than usual." The consequence is that smaller degrees of superiority tend to be judged as better with higher degrees of confidence, and that a certain slight degree of inferiority tends to be incorrectly judged as "better." We seem predisposed to judge "better" rather than "worse," and in this experiment the observers were, furthermore, predisposed in favor of the other person, somewhat more than in favor of themselves. They were disinclined to judge any trial as "worse than usual," and this disinclination was stronger when judging as witness than when judging as performer. This results in a combination of altruism and optimism which, if found to be a common occurrence, would seem to have interesting implications. Further investigation will perhaps show that these attitudes are conditioned, under different circumstances, by a variety of factors, such as competition, education, motive, age or sex of performer and witness, and perhaps by individual differences of a temperamental sort.

When Cattell had scientific men arrange their colleagues and themselves on the basis of scientific merit, he found no constant tendency either to overestimate or to underestimate oneself. He remarks, concerning this result: "It thus appears that there is no constant error in judging ourselves— we are about as likely to overestimate as to underestimate ourselves, and we can judge ourselves slightly more accurately than we are likely to be judged by one of our colleagues. We can only know ourselves from the reflected opinion of others, but it seems that we are able to estimate these more correctly than can those who are less interested. There are, however, wide individual differences; several observers overestimate themselves decidedly, while others underestimate themselves to an equal degree."[11]

Since these individual differences, in all the investigations that have been reported, are so conspicuous, we may next inquire whether the individual who possesses a given trait in high degree is a better or worse judge of that trait in himself and in others, than is a person in whom the trait itself is less marked.

III. Is one who possesses a given trait in high degree a better or worse judge of that trait than is an individual in whom the trait is less conspicuous? On the basis of the combined judgments of the group we have secured a final position for each individual, which indicates her most probable standing in the various traits. Since each individual judged all the others of the group, we can, by correlating[12] the judgments of each individual with the combined judgments of the group, secure a coefficient of correlation which will indicate the "judicial capacity" of the given individual. This figure will be a measure of the correctness or representative character of her judgments of her friends. If the figure is low, it will mean that her own judgments do not agree closely with the combined or true judgments. If the figure is high it will indicate that there is close correspondence, and that the individual's judgments of her friends agree closely with the combined judgment. Having secured these measures of judicial capacity, and having also measures of the degree to which each individual possesses the various traits, we may by correlating these two measures determine whether or not any relation exists between possession of the trait and ability to judge others with respect to that trait. In the same way we may determine the relation between possession of the trait and ability to judge oneself in that trait. The table on page 160 gives these coefficients of correlation in the case of all the traits.

In the cases of neatness, intelligence, humor, refinement and sociability the coefficients are all positive and fairly high. Thus in the case of humor the coefficients of .59 and .87 indicate that that individual whom others consider humorous tends to be the most correct or representative of the group in her judgments of the humor of herself and of others. The coefficients of .49 and .59 in the case of intelligence indicate that that individual who impresses others as being intelligent is a good judge of intelligence both in herself and in others. The same is to be said of neatness, refinement and sociability. In the case of beauty the coefficients, although positive, are very low and hence not very reliable. They seem to indicate that in this case there is no relation of any sort between the possession of the trait and the ability to judge it.

TABLE 5

Showing the Relation Between Possession of a Trait and Ability to Judge Self and Others in that Trait (All coefficients are positive unless otherwise indicated)

Trait	Judgment of Others	Judgment of Self	Trait	Judgment of Others	Judgment of Self
Neatness	.22	.45	Vulgarity	-.24	-.37
Intelligence	.49	.59	Snobbishness	.33	-.27
Humor	.59	.87	Conceit	.19	-.22
Beauty	.23	.15			
Refinement	.38	.83			
Sociability	.48	.47			

In the cases of the definitely "undesirable" traits, vulgarity, snobbishness and conceit, the coefficients tend to be negative, and although none of them is very high, they suggest that the possession of these traits to a given degree tends to disqualify the individual to that degree as a judge of those traits, whether in herself or in others. These results also confirm the results in the case of certain of the "desirable" traits, since vulgarity and snobbishness, with low or negative coefficients, are, grammatically at least, the opposites of refinement and sociability, which have high and positive coefficients.

In general, then, our results suggest that, in the case of "desirable" traits, ability to judge a quality accompanies possession of that quality, whereas in the case of the "undesirable" traits the reverse of this is the case.

IV. What relation exists between these estimated traits and the more objective measurements of the individuals concerned? On the basis of the mental tests we have secured measures which may be compared with these estimated traits. The same comparison may be made in the case of the academic records received by the individuals in their college courses. The following table shows the correlation of all the estimated traits with these two objective measurements.

TABLE 6

SHOWING THE RELATION BETWEEN ESTIMATED TRAITS AND (A) THE RESULTS OF MENTAL TESTS; (B) THE ACADEMIC RECORDS OF EACH INDIVIDUAL IN COLLEGE SUBJECTS

(All coefficients are positive unless otherwise indicated)

Trait	Correlation with Mental Tests	Correlation with Academic Record	Average
Intelligence	.62	.52	.57
Humor	.55	.15	.35
Refinement	.34	.34	.34
Snobbishness	.53	.13	.33
Neatness	.36	.24	.30
Conceit	.54	.03	.28

Beauty	.40	.06	.23
Sociability	.25	-.07	.09
Vulgarity	.29	-.31	-.01

In the case of the mental tests all the coefficients are positive and fairly high in most cases. The correlation is highest of all with estimated intelligence, whatever that may mean. As we have used the term it perhaps means the impression of general capacity which an individual makes on her associates. It is interesting to find that the mental tests, which can be administered in a few minutes, give us so close a measure of what this impression will be; a measure, it should be noted, which is higher than that afforded by the academic records, in spite of the fact that these academic records had been from term to term announced in a public way and might have been expected to contribute toward the general impression on the basis of which the judgments of intelligence were passed. The high correlation between tests and estimates suggests that the abilities displayed in these tests correspond very closely to those characteristics on which our associates base their estimates of our intelligence. This is an encouraging result for those interested in the vocational use of mental tests.

But it is equally interesting that the results of the mental test correlate to so high a degree with the estimates of various other traits, notably humor, snobbishness, conceit, beauty, neatness and refinement. This result suggests either or both of two interpretations. It may be, on the one hand, that these characteristics are only partial components of that more general trait, intelligence (with which the correlation of the tests is still higher), at least so far as the estimates of our associates are concerned. This would mean that a sense of humor, a tendency toward self-esteem, physical attractiveness and a gentle manner dispose one's associates to think favorably of her general mental endowment. On the other hand the result may mean that an individual who has sufficient distinction to stand out prominently in any of the estimated traits here considered is possessed of a nervous system which enables her to accomplish the work of these mental tests with corresponding efficiency. Such a characteristic as "general stand-out-ishness" may perhaps be a trait which calls for recognition, not only in daily life but also in the narrower categories of psychological classification.

In the case of the academic records this general tendency toward positive correlation is not present. The only high correlation is with estimated intelligence. It is impossible to say how far this high coefficient is due to general knowledge of academic attainments on the part of the individuals composing the groups. Refinement and neatness are the only other traits which show any claim at all for correlation with academic records. The positive direction of these coefficients may afford some consolation to those who put their faith in the vocational significance of academic records of college students, but their low values constitute a somewhat less encouraging commentary.

V. How do the various measures of intelligence compare with one another, and what is the reliability of these various measures? Frequent studies have been made of the relation between teachers' estimates of the general intelligence of pupils and their intelligence as shown by their performance in psychological tests. The teacher's estimate is perhaps very likely to be based on that sort of intelligence which shows itself in academic performance only, since in many cases the acquaintance is limited to contact in class room and laboratory. In our own case we have teachers' estimates only in the form of the actual class records. These are, then, not estimates of general intelligence in the strict sense, but are conditioned presumably for the most part by the student's performance in the class room.

The academic marks were reported according to a letter system, in which A means "very good," B means "good," C means "fair," D means "poor" and F means "failed." Having secured these marks for all the students in English, German, Logic, Psychology, Economics and History, we averaged the marks for each student, by giving A, B, C, D and F values of 90, 80, 70, 60 and 50. This gave us final averages for all the students, on the basis of which averages they were arranged in order of merit, the two groups being separately treated.

We have now the three following measures of intelligence:

      a. The results of the psychological tests.
      b. The opinion of fellow students.
      c. The academic records.

The correlations between these various measures are given in the following tabulation:

TABLE 7

SHOWING THE CORRELATIONS BETWEEN VARIOUS MEASURES OF INTELLIGENCE

	25 Juniors	25 Seniors
Correlation of psychological tests with estimated Intelligence	.70	.53
Correlation of psychological tests with Academic Records	.42	.57
Correlation of Academic Records with estimated Intelligence	.22	.37

The most striking result here is the rather low correlation of the academic records with the other measures of intelligence. The psychological tests agree closely with the results of the estimates by associates. The correlation of the tests with the records is considerably lower, while the correlation of records with estimates is exceedingly low. The full significance of these results will of course depend on the attitude one takes toward the various measures. One who has faith in the value of academic records must of course reject the estimates of associates and be very sceptical of the value of the mental tests. But vocationally the estimates of associates must always have value, since these determine or indicate the reactions of others toward a given individual, and vocational success will depend to a considerable degree on these reactions. The ultimate value of the mental tests is still to be determined; in fact, it was partly in order to aid in their evaluation that these experiments were performed. Inasmuch as the tests and the estimates agree closely, the tests and the records less closely, while the records do not correlate to any marked degree with either of the two other measures, the significance of the academic marks, or their reliability in this instance, must be seriously called into question.

TABLE 8

Trait	Correlation of Judicial Capacity and Ability in Mental Tests	Correlation of Judicial Capacity and Academic Records
Neatness	.05	.09
Intelligence	.55	.26
Humor	.48	-.02
Conceit	.20	.09
Beauty	.15	.14
Vulgarity	.18	.14
Snobbishness	.20	-.02
Refinement	.15	.25
Sociability	.26	.03

VI. Does the ability to judge the traits of others (judicial capacity) stand in any relation to proficiency in mental tests or to success in college work? The following table shows the correlation of judicial capacity in the case of each trait with standing in the tests and with academic records.

In the case of academic records there is seen to be absolutely no correlation with judicial capacity, in any of the traits estimated. In the case of the mental tests, only two of the traits yield high coefficients. In intelligence and in humor there is fairly high correlation (.55 and .48). The suggestion here is that those who do well in the mental tests are good judges of the intelligence and the humor of their friends, but that in the case of the other traits there is no necessary or probable relation.

Question VII. Is the individual who is a good judge of others also one whose self-estimates have high reliability? If the individuals are placed in an order of merit with respect to their judicial capacity in estimating the characteristics of their friends, and placed also in another order of merit on the basis of the accuracy of their self-estimates, what relation will be found between the two arrangements? The following table gives the coefficients of correlation when such arrangements are compared in the case of each of the traits.

TABLE 9

SHOWING THE RELATION BETWEEN ABILITY TO JUDGE OTHERS AND ABILITY TO JUDGE ONESELF

Trait	Correlation between Judicial Capacity and Accuracy of the Individual's Self-Estimates
Refinement	.54
Humor	.53
Beauty	.47
Sociability	.46
Intelligence	.44
Conceit	.26
Neatness	.22
Vulgarity	.22
Snobbishness	.15

All the coefficients are positive, their median value being .44. In the long run it is true that she who knows herself best is the best judge of others. The degree to which this is true, however, varies with the trait in question. With the "undesirable" traits of snobbishness, conceit and vulgarity, the coefficients are so low as to be quite unreliable and perhaps represent only chance. The same is true of neatness. But in the cases of refinement, humor, beauty, sociability and intelligence the coefficients are fairly high.

VIII. What correlations are found among various traits of character, as these are estimated by associates? For example, is an individual who is judged intelligent also likely to be judged to be humorous, or refined, or snobbish, etc.? If there are such correlations between estimated traits, what is their direction and amount? The following table shows the average correlations (from the two groups) in the case of all the traits:

TABLE 10

SHOWING THE INTERCORRELATION OR ESTIMATED TRAITS(1)

	Neat.	Intel.	Hum.	Con.	Beau.	Vulg.	Snob.	Refin.	Socia.
Neatness	—	.39	.29	.51	.50	.09	.57	.32	.10
Intelligence	.39	—	.59	.44	.34	.06	.43	.49	.25
Humor	.29	.59	—	.32	.50	.40	.50	.23	.55
Conceit	.51	.44	.32	—	.51	.24	.75	.33	.07
Beauty	.50	.34	.50	.51	—	-.09	.41	.56	.32
Vulgarity	.09	.06	.40	.24	-.09	—	.40	-.37	.18
Snobbishness	.57	.43	.50	.75	.41	.40	—	.20	-.12
Refinement	.32	.49	.23	.33	.56	-.37	.20	—	.34
Sociability	.10	.25	.55	.07	.32	.18	-.12	.34	—

[Note 1: The upper parts of this table and the one following repeat the figures given in the lower parts, for greater convenience in making comparisons and in presenting averages.]

Interesting as these coefficients are to one who has the passion for correlation, it is peculiarly difficult to state precisely what they mean. Neatness correlates, in varying degrees, with all the traits except vulgarity and sociability; intelligence with all except vulgarity and perhaps sociability; humor with all except neatness, conceit and refinement, where the coefficients are low; conceit correlates especially closely with neatness, beauty and snobbishness; beauty with neatness, humor, conceit and refinement; vulgarity correlates positively with only humor and snobbishness, and negatively with refinement; refinement, with everything except humor, snobbishness and vulgarity; snobbishness with all but refinement and sociability; while sociability correlates with nothing except humor. How far these figures measure definite relations between different and specific traits, how far they measure the degree to which one's impressions of various traits conspire to make up one's notion of other characteristics, or how far they measure only the degree of confusion that exists as to the precise meaning of the various words, it is exceedingly difficult to say.

IX. What degree of correlation exists among the academic records in the various college subjects? Is the individual who stands high in certain subjects likely to stand either high or low in other subjects or in all subjects? The following table shows the intercorrelations between eight subjects as calculated by the rather rough mode of grading and averaging previously described. Since the correlations are by the method of relative position, the fallacy of treating the various grades as susceptible of quantitative treatment is of very slight importance.

TABLE 11

SHOWING THE INTERCORRELATIONS AMONG GRADES IN EIGHT COLLEGE SUBJECTS, ON THE BASIS OF THE RECORDS OF THE 50 STUDENTS

	Psych.	Log.	Hist.	Econ.	Eng.	Germ.	Chem.	Math.	Avge.
Psychology	—	.60	.36	.52	.48	.49	.33	.54	.47
Logic	.60	—	.48	.57	.47	.41	.25	.57	.48
History	.36	.54	—	.44	.62	.46	.52	.61	.51
Economics	.52	.57	.44	—	.51	.43	.45	.71	.52
English	.48	.47	.62	.51	—	.25	.26	.46	.44
German	.49	.41	.46	.43	.25	—	.39	.38	.40
Chemistry	.33	.25	.52	.45	.26	.39	—	.57	.40
Mathematics	.54	.57	.61	.71	.46	.38	.57	—	.55

The correlations between the various college subjects are all positive, and argue against the commonly expressed belief in rather close specialization of abilities; the student who does well in one of these subjects tends to do well in all of them.

As has been frequently stated in this discussion, the data and conclusions here presented are by no means to be taken as final answers even to the specific questions asked. One cannot argue from what these groups of students do under the special conditions of this investigation to what they or others will do in other circumstances or in general. The results are presented mainly by way of suggesting the type of investigation which must be carried much further before we are in position to evaluate properly the self-analysis of an individual or the judgments of associates as presented in testimonials, interviews, or other indications based on general acquaintance. In the case of the psychological tests, a long program of selection, standardization, and accumulation of norms is laid out for those interested in the further advance of vocational psychology. So also from the point of view of introspective analysis, consultation, advice of friends, the methods of interview, testimonial, etc., there is an equally inviting though arduous program which must be carried through before even the most general principles of evaluation and selection are known.

It should also be insisted that the personal experience of this or that interviewer, adviser, teacher or expert is by no means a sufficient basis for general practice. Magic, clairvoyance, phrenology, physiognomics, were all founded on the treacherous basis of "personal observation" and occasional striking coincidence. Vocational psychology will be safe from prophets and charlatans only when it is made to rest on a stable structure of consistent and verifiable experimental data.

FOOTNOTES:

[9] See footnote on p. 42 for an explanation of the computation and meaning of such measures of deviation or error.

[10] Experimental Studies in Judgment, Archives of Psychology, No. 29, 1913, 119 pp.

[11] "American Men of Science." Second edition, p. 542.

[12] See p. 45 for explanation of the meaning and technique of correlation.

CHAPTER VIII

THE SCHOOL CURRICULUM AS A VOCATIONAL TEST

With certain qualifications the work of the school curriculum may be said to constitute an elaborate mental test. One important function of the curriculum is that of selecting and identifying individuals who possess a certain type of mental alertness or patience. Another function is that of supplying the individual with certain implements, facts and ideas, certain subject matter, which may or may not be of direct value in his later life but which is at least in this way perpetuated and preserved. A third function is that of affording opportunity for the exercise of such specific or general abilities as the curriculum may call into play.

All three of these functions have more or less direct vocational relevance. In the hands of industrial and technical interests, subject matter becomes more and more prominent as the important item. As this happens the older idea of discipline and exercise becomes subordinate or implicit. But, whatever be the underlying educational philosophy, the selective value of the curriculum is an inescapable fact. The public school system, by its processes of grading, promotion and certification, tends always to mark off as a distinct group those individuals who can and will meet its demands. It also attempts to differentiate the members of this group from one another on the basis of their ability or their inclination. The high schools, colleges, professional and technical courses continue this process of elimination, identification and selection. According to the student's ability and inclination to satisfy the requirements of the curriculum, he or she is dropped, graded, retarded, promoted or passed with honors.

Extending, as it commonly does, over many years of the individual's life, conducted by a considerable number and variety of examiners, and presented in a diversity of forms and methods, school work constitutes a type of mental test which is unequaled in its completeness. It is highly important for vocational psychology to ascertain the degree of correlation between the individual's record in the curriculum test and his success or fitness in later life. To what degree is the individual's academic record prognostic of his industrial, domestic and professional future?

As definite as this question is and as easy of solution as it may seem, it is only very recently that reliable data, as distinguished from unsupported opinions, have begun to be accumulated. The problem is complicated by the difficulty of securing satisfactory measures of success in later life, and by the difficulties encountered in following up the careers of those individuals whose early records are known. Shall success be measured by the obstacles overcome, the income earned, the sacrifices made, the social usefulness accomplished, the amount of local and contemporary publicity received, the public recognition accorded, the scope of activities attempted, or the historical eminence merited? And if more than one of these elements are to be considered, how are they to be treated commensurately? Certainly success may be achieved in any or several or all of these and other forms. For the present our information is limited to a few studies in which one or other of these aspects has been treated separately. As work in this field progresses we may be better able to sum up all the partial results into a statement of the general tendencies.

For our present purpose it may be best to bring together from various sources the data bearing on certain specific questions which have been propounded. At least three of these questions are distinctly relevant to the work of vocational psychology.

I. With respect to school work itself, what relation exists between the early success in elementary subjects and the later success in handling more advanced subject matter? This question is important to all those who may be concerned in advising individuals concerning the desirability and probable profit of continuing their school experience, and of entering occupations in which scholastic abilities may be requisite.

Kelley has recently reported a careful study of the relation between the marks in the fourth, fifth, sixth and seventh grades and the marks received in the first year of high school work. The results, in the case of fifty-nine pupils followed through the six years, were as follows:

Correlation between Marks in the Grades and Marks in First High School Year

7th grade .72
6th grade .73
5th grade .53
4th grade .62

His study further seeks to show the relative weight to be attributed to the work of each grade, by applying a formula known in statistics as a "regression equation." He says, "The net conclusion which may be drawn from these coefficients of correlation is that it is possible to estimate a person's general ability in the first year [H. S.] class from the marks he has received in the last four years of elementary school with accuracy represented by a coefficient of correlation of .789, and that individual idiosyncrasies may be estimated, in the case of mathematics and English, with an accuracy represented by a coefficient of correlation of .515.... Indeed, it seems that an estimate of a pupil's ability to carry high school work when the pupil is in the fourth grade may be nearly as accurate as a judgment given when the pupil is in the seventh grade."

Miles finds that the correlation between the average elementary school grade and the high school grade is .71. Dearborn also finds that high school efficiency is closely correlated with success in university work. He studied various groups of high school students, the groups containing from ninety-two to four hundred and seventy-two students each. These were grouped into quartiles on the basis of high school standing, and compared with similar classifications on the basis of university work. Dearborn summarizes his results in the following words:

"We may say then, on the basis of the results secured in this group (472 pupils) which is sufficiently large to be representative, that if a pupil has stood in the first quarter of a large class through high school the chances are four out of five that he will not fall below the first half of his class in the university.... The chances are but about one in five that the student who has done poorly in high school—who has been in the lowest quarter of his class —will rise above the median or average of the freshman class at the university, and the chances that he will prove a superior student at the university are very slim indeed.... The Pearson coefficient of correlation of the standings in the high schools and in the freshman year, for this group of 472 pupils, is .80.... A little over 80 per cent of those who were found in the lowest or the highest quarter of the group in high school are found in their respective halves of the group throughout the university.... Three-fourths of the students who enter the university from these high schools will maintain throughout the university approximately the same rank which they held in high school."

Lowell's investigation, which is discussed in later paragraphs, also bears directly on the question of the relation between college entrance records, college grades, and later work in professional schools. A rather different method of procedure was adopted by Van Denburg, who studied the relation between the first-term marks of high school pupils in New York City and the length of time the pupils continued in school work. The following table gives a general idea of his results:

TABLE 12

Showing the Relation between First-term Marks in High School and the Length of Time Pupils Remain in School (Van Denburg)

First-Term Mark	Percentage Leaving School in Various Years After Entrance into the High School		
	Left During First Year	Left in 2nd, 3rd, or 4th Years, or Failed to Graduate in 4th	Graduated
Below 50%	61	39	0
50 to 59%	49	46	5
60 to 69%	39	58	3
70 to 79%	20	62	18
80 to 89%	17	46	37
90 to 100%	6	40	54

Thorndike, in referring to the significance of such results, says: "Ten times as many of those marked below 50 leave in the first year as of those marked 90 or above. Of 115 pupils marked below 50 not one remained to graduate in four years. As the marks rise the percentage leaving in the early years steadily falls and the percentage graduating rises. Such prophecies... could easily be worked out for any community. They show that in the important matter of the length of stay in school a pupil's career is far from being a matter of unpredictable fortuity.... It will not be long before [we] will remember with amusement the time when education waited for the expensive tests of actual trial to tell how well a boy or girl would succeed with a given trade, with the work of college and professional school, or with the general task of leading a decent, law-abiding, humane life."

Prompted by Dearborn's study of the relation between work in high school and work in the university, Smith made a somewhat more intensive study of a group of students in the University of Iowa. Dearborn had investigated the academic careers of pupils from eight large and four small high schools in Wisconsin, and concluded that three-fourths of the students entering the university from these high schools would maintain throughout the university approximately the same rank as they had held in high school. When the groups were divided into upper and lower halves, about seventy per cent of those in the upper high school section were found in the upper half of the university section; about the same number of those in the lower high school half were found in the lower university half.

Smith's data showed almost precisely the same figures as those of Dearborn. From the Liberal Arts class of 1910 (one hundred and sixty students) those were chosen whose records were complete in both high school and university. This gave a total of one hundred and twenty students. On the basis of their standing, as based on the grades assigned in all subjects studied, they were ranked in order for each year of high school and university. They were then separated into quintiles on the basis of these rankings, and their standing in these various quintiles observed from year to year.

When the students, on the basis of their general high school average (for the four years), are distributed through their respective quintiles in the university (general average again) the results are as shown in the table on page 183.

TABLE 13

SHOWING THE RELATIONS BETWEEN HIGH SCHOOL RECORDS AND UNIVERSITY RECORDS (SMITH). *See Text for Explanation*

H. S. Average	University Average				
	1st Quint.	2nd Quint.	3rd Quint.	4th Quint.	5th Quint.
1st Quintile	54%	17%	17%	4%	8%
2nd Quintile	25%	29%	17%	13%	16%
3rd Quintile	17%	25%	20%	21%	17%
4th Quintile	0%	25%	25%	33%	17%
5th Quintile	4%	4%	21%	29%	42%

In considering this table it is apparent that if the high school students were distributed through the various university quintiles on a purely chance basis, and without any reference to their high school records, there would tend to be twenty per cent of each high school quintile in each of the university quintiles. Any percentage higher than this twenty per cent thus indicates some significant relation between the two sets of grades. On the whole there is a close relation indicated. The tendency is clear for those in a given high school quintile to be found in or near the same quintile in their university work. The relation is particularly close in the highest and lowest quintiles. In the intermediate quintiles there is more or less shifting about.

In the same way it is possible to classify all students in quintiles during their first high school year, and then to trace their careers through the following three years of high school and four years of college. The following tabulation shows the results when this was done. The figures show the percentage of each quintile in first year high school who were found in the same quintile in the various later years.

TABLE 14

SHOWING THE RELATION BETWEEN RECORDS IN THE FIRST HIGH SCHOOL YEAR, AND RECORDS IN SUBSEQUENT YEARS IN HIGH SCHOOL AND COLLEGE (SMITH)

	High School				University			
Quintiles	1	2	3	4	1	2	3	4
First	100%	70%	67%	67%	52%	36%	43%	25%

Second	100%	54%	33%	29%	35%	33%	22%	8%
Third	100%	41%	37%	21%	35%	20%	22%	21%
Fourth	100%	29%	25%	21%	48%	28%	17%	25%
Fifth	100%	50%	59%	50%	45%	32%	39%	38%
Averages	100%	49%	44%	38%	43%	30%	29%	23%

Here again, if the subsequent distributions were on a chance basis with respect to the first year high school grades, there would tend to be but twenty per cent in each of the various quintiles. As a matter of fact, the percentages never fall so low as twenty per cent, although in the senior college year they approach very close to this figure.

It is to be noted that changes so small as from one quintile to the immediately adjacent one are not taken into account in this table. The figures show only those who were in precisely the same quintile all the way through. The indication is then that a student's performance in the first high school year is very significant of what his performance will be through the rest of the high school course, and also of significance with respect to what he will do in his university work. The significance of the early work, as has appeared in other studies also, becomes less and less the farther through the course one goes, so that in the senior year in college there is approximately a chance distribution with reference to the work of the first year high school.

Smith also presents his results in the form of coefficients of correlation between various rankings. The following are the most interesting in the present connection:

TABLE 15

CORRELATIONS (SMITH)

H. S. Average and Univ. Freshman Average   .48

H. S. Average and Univ. Sophomore Average .39

H. S. Average and Univ. Junior Average   .47

H. S. Average and Univ. Senior Average   .28

1st and 2nd Year High School	.77
1st and 3rd Year High School	.67
1st and 4th Year High School	.66
University Freshman and Sophomore	.73
University Freshman and Junior	.61
University Freshman and Senior	.45

These figures of course indicate the same facts as those derived from the previous methods of expressing the data. The high school (H. S.) average correlates throughout with the college ranking, the correspondence becoming less apparent in the later college years. Similarly, the good students in the first high school year are the good ones all through the high school course, and the able college freshmen are able as sophomores, juniors and seniors. But both in high school and in college the significance of early standing becomes less and less as the years progress.

A. L. Jones[13] compared college entrance examinations with work done later in the college course, in the freshman and sophomore years. Two hundred men from the entering classes of 1907, 1911 and 1912, in Columbia College, were selected for study. These men were arranged in four groups, fifty in each group, on the basis of (a) their marks in entrance examinations, (b) their college marks in the first and second college years. Group I contains the best fifty individuals, Group II the fifty next best, etc. The following compiled table shows where the members of each group in entrance examinations stood in their college work:

TABLE 16

SHOWING RELATIONS BETWEEN ENTRANCE RECORDS AND COLLEGE STANDING (JONES)

See Text for Explanation

	On Basis of Freshman Ranking			
On Basis of Entrance Examinations	Group I	Group II	Group III	Group IV

Group I (50 men)	30	13	5	2
Group II (50 men)	16	17	12	5
Group III (50 men)	3	13	16	18
Group IV (50 men)	1	7	17	25
On Basis of Entrance Examinations	On Basis of Sophomore Ranking			
Group I (13 men)	7	4	2	0
Group II (13 men)	4	5	2	2
Group III (13 men)	2	4	3	4
Group IV (14 men)	0	0	6	8

It appears from this table that there is a fairly well-marked tendency for the men to remain in the group in which they start. At least the larger number of men are found in college in about the same group in which they occurred on the basis of entrance examinations. Jones writes, "It is evident from an examination of these... data that entrance examinations, aside from other important uses claimed for them by their advocates, may fitly be taken as an important indication of the future career of the candidate for admission. They should of course be supplemented, and so should any other means of determining preparation for college. Those who have studied the question tell us that there is a high degree of correlation between intellectual qualities and others. A good test of intellectual fitness is, therefore, in some degree a test of other qualities also. Entrance examinations have their imperfections but there can be no doubt that they may serve as a solid foundation on which to build."

Thorndike, on the other hand, in studying the relation between entrance marks and later college standing (Columbia College classes entering in 1901, 1902 and 1903), finds results which lead him to say, "The important facts concerning the relationship of success in entrance examinations to success in college work... prove that we cannot estimate the latter from the former with enough accuracy to make the entrance examinations worth taking or to prevent gross and intolerable injustice being done to many individuals.... The records of eleven entrance examinations give a less accurate prophecy of what a student will do in the latter half of his college course than does the college record of his brother! The correlation between brothers in intellectual ability is approximately .40, but that between standing in entrance examinations and standing in college of the same person is only .47 for junior year (130 cases) and .25 for senior year (56 cases).... From many facts such as these... it is certain that the traditional entrance examinations, even when as fully safeguarded as in the case of those given by the College Entrance Examination Board, do not prevent incompetence from getting into college; do not prevent students of excellent promise from being discouraged or barred out altogether; do not measure fitness for college well enough to earn the respect of students or teachers; and do intolerable injustice to individuals."

The apparent striking contradiction between these two reports is not, however, so serious when it is noted that the records of Jones were taken from freshman and sophomore years, while Thorndike's, as here quoted, were taken from junior and senior years. Thorndike has also presented, in another connection, comparisons of entrance examinations with the work of freshman and sophomore years, and in these cases his correlations are considerably higher, more nearly approximating the results of Jones. The correlations, for the four college years, were as follows: freshman year, .62; sophomore year, .50; junior year, .47; senior year, .25.

Apparently the only safe conclusion at present is that the entrance examinations are fairly useful in predicting the early college work, their prognostic value becoming less and less as the interval between the two measures is increased. This result is of course to be expected. In another section of this book occasion is taken to show that preliminary trials are of little value in indicating the relative abilities of individuals when they have reached or approximated their limit of practice.

II. Are the school subjects in which one is most interested in any way an indication of the interests and values of later life? What, in general, are the facts concerning the permanence of interests and the relation between interest and ability? These questions are of immediate interest to parents, teachers and vocational counsellors.

Here again we must turn to the work of Thorndike for almost the only available information, and even this is only preliminary and tentative, the results being subject to various sources of error. This investigator studied the interests and abilities in mathematics, history, literature, science, music, drawing and manual work. The original records are the judgments of one hundred individuals concerning the order of their own interests and abilities in these subjects at each of three periods in their school career, elementary school, high school and college. These various judgments having been made as conscientiously as possible, correlations were determined between interests at different times, interests and abilities, etc.

Individual relative interests at different times, according to these records, do not vary according to mere caprice. "A correlation of .60 or .70 seems to be approximately the true degree of resemblance between the relative degree of an interest in a child of from ten to fourteen and the same person at twenty-one." The resemblance between ability in elementary years and ability in college is found to be .65. The correlation between interest in the last three years of elementary school and capacity in the college period is computed to be about .60. This would mean that the early interest would serve as a useful indicator of adult capacity. "The correlation between an individual's order of subjects for interest and his order for ability is one of the closest of any that are known (about .90)." "A person's relative interests are an extraordinarily accurate symptom of his relative capacities."

In concluding his report Thorndike writes, "Interests are shown to be [not only permanent but also] symptomatic, to a very great extent, of present and future capacity or ability. Either because one likes what he can do well, or because one gives zeal and effort to what he likes, or because interest and ability are both symptoms of some fundamental feature of the individual's original nature, or because of the combined action of all three of these factors, interest and ability are bound very close together. The bond is so close that either may be used as a symptom for the other almost as well as for itself. The importance of these facts for the whole field of practice with respect to early diagnosis, vocational guidance, the work of social secretaries, deans, advisers, and others who direct students' choices of schools, studies, and careers is obvious. They should be taken account of in such practice until they are verified or modified by data obtained by a better method; and such data should soon be collected. The better method is, of course, to get the measurements of relative interest and of relative ability, not from memory, but at the time, and not from individuals' reports alone, but by objective tests."

III. Is there any relation between general or particular academic aptitude or inclination and general or particular proficiency in the later domestic, industrial, commercial, professional or civic activities? This question is of importance not only to the individual and his guide but also to employers, agencies and society at large.

An interesting and significant study bearing on this question has been reported by Nicholson, who investigated the relation between academic success and prominence in later life. The men graduating from Wesleyan University during the years 1833 to 1899, 1,667 in number, were arranged in three groups. In the first group were the 140 "honor" men, who were valedictorians or salutatorians of their classes. In the second group were placed all the men elected to Phi Beta Kappa, on the basis of high scholarship. Of these there were 461. In the third group were placed the remaining 1,206 men. It was then determined how many of these men were found in the current edition of *Who's Who,* or were judged, by faculty or fellow students, as having been or about to be of sufficient distinction to be included in such a directory. The results are given in the following tabulation.

TABLE 17

SHOWING THE RELATION BETWEEN COLLEGE HONORS AND INCLUSION IN *Who's Who* (NICHOLSON)

See Text for Explanation

643 Students, of the years 1833-1859	Per Cent Judged by Faculty to be of *Who's Who* Rank
Honor Men (53)	50
P.B.K. Men (167)	32
Remainder (476)	6
604 Students of the Years 1860-1889	Per Cent Found in 1914-15 Edition of *Who's Who*
Honor Men (59)	48

P.B.K. Men (185)	31
Remainder (419)	10
420 Students of the Years 1890-1899	Per Cent in Who's Who or Judged by Classmates as about to be There.
Honor Men (28)	50
P.B.K. Men (109)	30
Remainder (311)	11
Total of 1667 Students	Per Cent with Distinction Entitling to Inclusion in *Who's Who*.
Honor Men (140)	50
P.B.K. Men (461)	31
Remainder (1206)	9

Referring to these results, Nicholson remarks, "From this study of the careers of sixteen hundred and sixty-seven graduates, living and dead, where three different methods are employed in determining distinction in after life, it appears that the results are fairly constant, and we are justified in assuming that, for this college at least, the chances of distinction for a high honor graduate, one of the two or three leading scholars of the class, are just even; that one out of three of those elected to Phi Beta Kappa is likely to achieve pronounced success in life; and that each of the remaining members of the class has less than one chance in ten to become famous. In other words, roughly speaking, the quarter (or the fifth) of the class elected to Phi Beta Kappa are likely to supply just as many distinguished men as are the remaining three-quarters (now four-fifths) of the class."

The study of Nicholson includes only that type of success which would be likely to lead to inclusion in *Who's Who*, viz., the more strictly literary, professional, political, and academic success. The commercial, industrial and business careers are not so likely to lead to inclusion in this directory, and yet success in them is no less definite than in the professional work. It is rather difficult to determine the degree to which success in these fields is determined by ability alone, and to what degree it is a function of chance, inheritance, social charm, prestige, and geographical and economic circumstance. Nevertheless it would be interesting to know whether such measure of success as can be secured correlates in any way with success in the work of school years.

In an unpublished study of the graduates of Pratt Institute, Dr. D. E. Rice has compared the grades achieved by students in the courses in Mechanical Engineering and Electrical Engineering with the salaries the men were receiving several years after graduation. There were in all six classes of men, numbering about forty each—three classes from Mechanical Engineering and three from Electrical Engineering, for the years of 1907, 1908, 1909. The salary reports were asked for in 1913, four to six years after graduation.

The men were ranked according to the grades they received in the eight different subjects included in the curriculum, the grades being 10, 9, 8, and 7, corresponding to the ordinary grade system of A, B, C, D. They were then ranked according to the salary reported at the time of the investigation. Results for each class were treated separately so that the time elapsing since graduation was not a factor in the results. The following table gives the results when these two rankings were correlated by two statistical methods of computing correlation.

In every case the correlation between grades and salary is positive, although the coefficients are all small. This means that in the long run there is a general tendency for the good salaries to go to the men whose grades were high, but that there are many exceptions to the rule. Certainly in no class is the opposite tendency shown, for the good salaries to go to the poor students. It is probable that the correlations found here are as low as they are partly because in this technical school there is no special effort made to encourage high grades for their own sake, the emphasis being rather on getting a good average rating.

TABLE 18

SHOWING THE CORRELATION BETWEEN SCHOOL STANDING AND SALARIES EARNED IN LATER LIFE (RICE)

See Text for Explanation

Class and Year	Cases	Correlation by Pearson Method, and P.E.	Correlation by Per Cent of Unlike Signs, and P.E.
Mechanical '07	35	.36 .08	.22 .09
Mechanical '08	41	.25 .09	.34 .08
Mechanical '09	39	.21 .09	.06 .10
Electrical '07	26	.16 .13	.25 .12
Electrical '08	36	.46 .08	.51 .08
Electrical '09	41	.16 .10	.28 .09
Averages		.267	.277

Just what these degrees of correlation mean is made somewhat more apparent if we treat the data in another way. If instead of computing coefficients of correlation we divide each class of men into four quartiles, and determine the average salaries of the men in these quartiles, we get very definite results. The upper quartile or group will now contain that fourth of the class whose grades were highest. The second, third and fourth quartiles will in turn represent decreasing degrees of academic proficiency. If the average salaries are the same for all quartiles, this will mean that there is no relation between salary and school grades. But if the salary varies with the grades, this will be a significant result. The actual data are as follows:

TABLE 19

Rice's Data Presented in a Revised Form

		Average Salaries of the			
Class and Year	Cases	1st Quartile	2nd Quartile	3rd Quartile	4th Quartile
Mechanical '07	35	$1800	$1675	$1362	$1387
Mechanical '08	41	1450	1512	1512	1275
Mechanical '09	39	1375	1262	1313	1137
Electrical '07	26	1750	1675	1675	1412
Electrical '08	36	2147	1437	1262	1262
Electrical '09	41	1462	1212	1387	1200

Averages		$1664	$1462	$1418	$1279
Percentages		100%	87%	85%	76%

If the separate classes be now considered the results are seen to be more or less irregular, although the general tendency is apparent. If the average results from all six classes are considered the results are more reliable as well as more uniform. The average salary varies in the same way as do the grades. If the average salary of the men of the first quartile ($1,664) be taken as a basis of comparison and considered one hundred per cent, then the salaries of the men in the second, third and fourth quartiles are respectively only eighty-seven, eighty-five and seventy-six per cent of this amount. In general terms, the salary of the men in the lower or poorest quarter of the class, from the point of view of school grades, will be only three-fourths the salary of the men in the upper or best quarter. The two middle quartiles will differ but little from each other, although the second has the advantage, by two per cent, or $44, over the third quarter.

If the class be divided into a better and a poorer half, then the average salary of the men in the upper half is seen to be $1,563, while that of the men in the lower half is only $1,348. The men in the upper half earn $215 more in a year than the men in the lower half. This way of expressing the results is both clearer and more concrete than the mere statement of the coefficient of correlation.

Interesting data on all three of these preceding questions are to be found in A. Lawrence Lowell's study of the academic careers of students in Harvard College, Law School and Medical School. This investigation included an examination into the college entrance examinations, the records attained during the college course, the subjects elected in this course, and the subsequent achievement of the men in the professional schools of law and medicine. The statistics cover the cases of all men who took the degree of A. B. at Harvard and then graduated from the two professional schools connected with Harvard. Only men who had taken at least three years of college work in residence were included. The records for the Law School cover the twenty years from 1891 to 1910. Those for the Medical School cover the sixteen years from 1895 forward.

The college gives degrees indicating four grades of distinction on the basis of scholarship. These are indicated as "plain," "cum laude," "magna cum laude" and "summa cum laude." The two professional schools grant degrees with two grades of distinction, viz., "plain" and "cum laude."

Lowell assumes that the grade attained on the college entrance examinations indicates with a certain degree of correctness the natural scholarly abilities of the student. The course of studies elected during college reflects roughly the general interests of the student at that time. The college records indicate his ability in the pursuit of those studies, including under ability such things as persistence, patience, fidelity, zeal, as well as native intelligence. The records in the professional schools are taken as indicating quite approximately the student's real ability to achieve success in the particular professional work of the technical sort.

All students are consequently classified according to these various factors. The entrance examinations are divided into "clear" and "conditioned." The college degrees and the professional degrees are classified on the basis of the degree of distinction awarded. All students are also classified on the basis of their election of the four possible college courses: (a) literature and languages; (b) natural sciences; (c) history and political science; (d) philosophy and mathematics. The relations between these various classifications are then presented, and analyzed in various ways.

Thus it is shown that there is very little or no relation between the college course elected and the probability of achieving a degree "cum laude" in the professional schools. The figures are summed up in the following table:

TABLE 20

Showing Relation between Course Elected in College and Honors Received in Subsequent Years in Professional Schools (Lowell)

Course Pursued	Degree in Law School		Degree in Medical School	
	Plain	"Cum Laude"	Plain	"Cum Laude"
Lit. and Lang.	801	180 (18.4%)	145	166 (53.4%)
Nat. Science	19	3 (13.6%)	75	81 (51.9%)

Hist. and Pol. Sci.	627	129 (17.1%)	30	20 (44.4%)
Phil. and Math	8	11 (57.9%)	6	7 (53.8%)

The figures suggest that "as a preparation for the study of law or medicine it makes comparatively little difference what subject is mainly pursued in college." That is to say, college interests in natural sciences, as indicated by the election of that course, does not indicate special aptitude for the work of medicine; nor does the election of courses in history and political science indicate a necessary superiority in the more or less related work of law. Lowell shows that only during the first year or so of the medical school do those who have already specialized in natural sciences have any advantage over those medical students who have specialized in other subjects.

What is the relation between the men's records in college and their achievement in the professional schools? In the following table are given the number of college men of each degree of distinction who were awarded "cum laude" in the professional schools:

TABLE 21

Showing Relation between College Honors and Honors in the Professional Schools (Lowell)

Record in College	Number Awarded "Cum Laude" in Law
609 Plain Degree	40 6.6%
305 Cum Laude	68 22.3%
200 Magna Cum Laude	80 40.0%
33 Summa Cum Laude	20 60.0%
Record in College	Number Awarded "Cum Laude" in Medicine
239 Plain	86 36.0%
85 Cum Laude	65 76.5%
39 Magna Cum Laude	34 87.2%
2 Summa Cum Laude	2 100.0%

It is apparent at once that there is a close relation between the college records and the records in the professional schools. Both in law and in medicine those who are awarded honors tend largely to be those who were awarded honors in college. And the higher the college honors, the greater the percentage of men receiving honors in the professional schools.

We may now ask how far back in the academic careers of these men it is possible to predict their probable achievement in the professional schools. Have those who are awarded the professional honors already distinguished themselves from their fellows at the time of their entrance into college? The following summary of the results presented by Lowell in much more detail will help answer this question:

TABLE 22

SHOWING RELATIONS BETWEEN VARIOUS ACADEMIC RECORDS (LOWELL)

Men Graduating from the Law School and Receiving "Cum Laude" in Law

	Per cent
Entered college "clear"	26.4
Entered college "conditioned"	9.0
Graduated from college with distinction	31.2
Graduated from college without distinction	6.5
Entrance clear and college distinction	37.9
Entrance conditioned and college with distinction	18.1
Entrance clear and college without distinction	11.1
Entrance conditioned and college without distinction	2.9

Men Graduating from the Medical School and Receiving "Cum Laude" in Medicine

	Per cent
Entered college "clear"	59.1

Entered college "conditioned"	43.0
Graduated from college with distinction	80.1
Graduated from college without distinction	36.0
Entrance clear and college distinction	78.1
Entrance conditioned and college distinction	84.6
Entrance clear and college without distinction	42.4
Entrance conditioned and college without distinction	31.4

Here the result is clearly suggested that early merit in academic work means success in the professional schools, whether one considers entrance examinations or college records. And the most probable group for professional honors is made up of those men who combined both entrance and college distinction. This is especially striking in the case of the law school. In the case of the medical school the differences are not quite so great, although the general tendency is quite the same. This is said to be due to the lower standard required for medical honors during these years. Lowell concludes: "The men who are destined to take the highest rank in the law and medical schools are markedly better scholars, both in the preparatory schools and in college, than their fellows. In intellectual power, as in other things, the boy is father to the man."

On the whole, then, all these studies point in a consistent direction; those who are destined to achieve distinction and success begin to do so at an early age. Whether measured by achievement in academic courses, honors in professional and technical courses, salary earned after graduation, or inclusion among lists and directories of eminent men, success in later life is suggested by success in the early work of the school curriculum. In spite of frequent comments to the contrary, the school curriculum would seem to constitute a useful test in prognosticating at least the most probable quality of the individual's later work.

But our original three questions are at present answered with very unequal reliability. With respect to the relation between early success or failure in elementary school subjects and success or failure in handling more advanced subject matter, the evidence is clear and definite.

On the question as to the permanence of interests and the relation between interest and ability, the evidence is far from adequate for vocational purposes. While the conclusion suggested is positive in Thorndike's study, the investigator recognizes that the results require confirmation or refutation at the hands of more reliable and verifiable information. It has appeared fairly certain that interest, as reflected in choice of college subjects, bears no relation to ability to undertake the work of at least two definite branches of professional training.

On the third question, concerning the relation between general or particular academic aptitude or inclination and general or particular proficiency in later domestic, industrial, commercial, professional or civic activities, the data, although consistent, are far from complete. Here, then, as in so many other aspects of vocational psychology, we find an inviting field of research and an abundance of interesting problems.

FOOTNOTES:

[13] *Educational Review*, September, 1914.

CHAPTER IX

THE DETERMINANTS OF VOCATIONAL APTITUDE

Without attempting to distinguish between the different detailed occupations, either on the basis of materials dealt with, the social or individual purposes realized, or the special qualifications demanded, we can still divide vocations broadly into five general types, depending on the degree to which they are likely to call for complete and normal psychological equipment. Such a classification is of little service in the concrete guidance of individuals, since the general types include work of the most diverse sorts; but it may be useful in suggesting the various types of qualities that are of vital importance in determining aptitude for any work at all, and may in this way aid in outlining the work of further investigation.

1. In the first place there are many useful and remunerative types of labor which can be performed by a domesticated animal or an imbecile, when working under constant or close supervision. Hauling loads, mowing grass, felling timber, sawing wood, digging holes, breaking stone, weaving doormats, and the simple types of work commonly performed in institutions for the mentally deficient are instances. The detection of individuals thus poorly equipped, their congregation and segregation under supervision, and their useful employment, are at once psychologically easy and economically desirable, as has already been indicated in detail in Chapter III.

2. Somewhat more abundant and diversified are those forms of employment for the unspecialized mental competent. This requires only a sufficient degree of intelligence to enable the individual to escape classification as a mental incompetent. One who is capable of earning a living under favorable circumstances, in the absence of aggressive competition and without close supervision, can find his or her level in the "blind alley" occupations. These offer no prospects of promotion to positions of responsibility and skill, and by definition, this group of individuals afford suitable workers for these

occupations. They fill the gap between the feeble-minded and that degree of intelligence which the most moderately endowed *average* individual typifies. Rough clerking and attending, simple personal and domestic service, delivering goods of small value, laundry work of the mechanical sort, supervised manual and agricultural labor, waiting on domesticated animals, standardized and mechanical factory operations, wrapping, cleaning, polishing, petty shop-keeping, running errands and freight elevators, street cleaning, janitorial assistance, etc., are forms of work about equally difficult and satisfying. They do not involve the acquisition of special skill or technical knowledge and they are capable of performance, in the main, by almost any physically able person above the status of feeble-mindedness. We may expect that in the very near future there will be provided standardized scales for the determination of general intelligence of this degree. Even now it is fairly easy to select from a group of children those who, while not positively mentally defective, are nevertheless slow of comprehension, stupid, unable to acquire new knowledge and skill with facility, and perhaps disinclined or unable to form the moral and social habits of honesty, cleanliness, promptness, truthfulness and economy. Since these can fill the "blind alley" occupations with fair satisfaction they should be "guided" into the first available positions of this kind.

Thorndike has advocated a series of tests, experience with which leads him to say:

"Suppose that the general intellectual ability of the dullest men who are able to support and look after themselves (men who though temperate and strong earn say $400 a year in good times in New York City) be represented by a and that of Aristotle or Goethe by $a+b$, the difference, b, being 100. Then the amount of such ability assigned by the tests alone would not, on the average, vary from the individual's true amount by more than 5; and would not vary therefrom by more than 14 in one case out of a hundred. The 5 and 14 are very cautious estimates, 4 and 11 being probably nearer what such an experiment would in fact reveal."

He further remarks, "There is excellent reason to believe that it is literally true that the result of two hours' tests properly chosen from those already tested gives a better diagnosis of an educated adult's general intellectual ability than the result of the judgments of two teachers or friends who have observed him in the ordinary course of life each for a thousand hours."[14] Interesting applications of tests of this general character have been reported by Scott. Workers of various kinds, such as salesmen and clerks, were graded by their employers or supervisors on the basis of their actual ability at their task. It was possible in some cases to get very accurate objective measures of ability to sell goods, etc., by keeping records of achievement over a considerable period of time. These objective measures have been compared with the results of psychological tests administered at the time the men were employed. Positive correlations ranging in several instances as high as .80 to .90 were secured. This means that ability in the performance of the particular mental tests used was a very reliable sign of ability in the field. Various instances similar to these have already been described in Chapter 5.

3. If, as seems quite likely, it be ultimately demonstrated that there are some characteristics, aptitudes and capacities that depend directly on congenital endowment, special nervous and sensory characteristics of a valuable kind, we may mark off another group of occupations for which particular individuals are well adapted, though not exclusively so, by original nature. Among the traits which have been said to occur in some such direct hereditary way, or as the result of unexplained mutation or deviation from type, are: mathematical aptitude, ability in drawing, musical composition, singing, poetic reaction, military strategy, chess playing. Maternity, as a vocation, is of course strictly sex limited. Pitch discrimination seems to depend on structural factors which are not susceptible of improvement by practice. The same may be said of various forms of professional athletic achievement. Color blindness seems to be an instance of the conspicuous absence of such a unit characteristic. "Poets," it is said, "are born, not made." Many of these apparent unit characteristics are so relatively independent that they often occur in quite surprising degree in individuals who are otherwise imbecilic. Mathematical, musical, graphic and decorative aptitudes, mechanical memory, and certain types of manual dexterity and mechanical cunning are frequently exhibited by the *idiot savant*. By the *idiot savant* is meant an individual who is in most respects mentally defective, who perhaps cannot dress himself, cannot adequately learn to speak or write, but who possesses some particular ability to a surprising degree. Such individuals may be able to perform on various musical

instruments, to compose music, to sketch designs and objects in an imitative manner, to remember long lists of disconnected names or numbers, to weave acceptably such articles as rugs and scarfs, or to construct complicated mechanical objects such as furniture, pumps, and sailing vessels.

Cases of rare possession of unit characters constitute the "genius" of ordinary conversation. These seem to present no problem for vocational psychology. Their marked unusualness renders them sufficiently obvious, even to the individual who does not systematically analyze himself. Such a prodigy requires a generous friend and an opportunity rather than a vocational expert.

4. There remain two further types of work, in which vocational psychology really finds its true task. There are on the one hand a large number of occupations that require neither unusual intelligence, special aptitude, nor technical training, such as those of the small tradesmen, responsible clerks, collectors, watchmen, agents, solicitors, motormen, conductors, soldiers, cashiers, cooks, nursemaids, etc. Above all, these types of work require the moral and social virtues, such as honesty, courtesy, truthfulness, patience, promptness, cleanliness, etc. Their lack of need of special technical knowledge is indicated by the apprenticeship method by which most of them are commonly begun. Also, the absence of simple and direct tests of the presence of these moral and social virtues and habits requires that for a long time to come this method of trial, combined with the judgments of associates in the form of testimonial, personal recommendation, etc., must be continued. If psychology, in the immediate or remote future, shall ever discover or invent expedient tests for the measurements of these moral characteristics, it will have done a work that is at present equaled only by the formation of the various graded scales for measuring more strictly intellectual capacities. At present no such tests are vouched for by even the most enthusiastic of prophets.

5. Finally, and closely related to these occupations calling mainly for moral habits and social reactions, come the bulk of the world's occupations, those adequately performed by and constituting the permanent task of the man or woman of average intelligence. By average intelligence we do not of course imply any uniform or standardized homogeneous equipment. We mean

those varying degrees of intellectual proficiency, educative docility, social coöperativeness and instinctive adequacy which fill the major section of the curve of distribution, that between the feeble-minded and obviously stupid, on the one hand, and on the other the genius, with special and distinguished traits or capacities.

In these occupations the degree of intelligence is by no means the sole determinant of either successful or satisfactory performance. Temperamental characteristics, such as those enumerated by Schneider and by Thorndike, the local and wandering inclinations, active and sedentary dispositions, tendencies to competitiveness, imitation, suggestibility, sympathy, curiosity, and the entire series of instinctive propensities, dominant original or acquired types of satisfaction and annoyance, attitudinal, volitional and emotional differences, and the moral and social traits, such as persistence, frankness, piety, loyalty, zeal, all these may be expected to combine in varying relations of compensation and reënforcement, substitution and facilitation. What one lacks in quickness it is often possible to make up in persistence; what another lacks in ambition and competitiveness he may supply in the form of loyalty and zeal; relative intellectual inferiority is often and easily balanced by the display of social charm; persistent, well-directed and enthusiastic effort or even a good vocabulary may enable one to compete successfully with the exceptional genius who does not display these incentives or advantages.

In the proposals to direct individuals into their proper life careers, the advocates have quite commonly failed to make sufficient allowance for the overwhelming importance of incentive, motive, attitude and purpose, and the large rôle they play in determining the possible achievements of a nervous system. It is well enough to test the memory span, attention type, and reaction time of an applicant for a job as motorman on a street car. It is still more important to learn the strength of his instinctive competitive reactions, to measure the degree of his belief in hell or in socialism, or the firmness of his intention to effect the higher education of his children. By "more important" I mean better calculated to reveal his fitness for the work. I would rather trust my life and limb to a motorman whose feeble memory span is reënforced by a loyal devotion to the comfort of his grandmother than to a mnemonic prodigy whose chief actuating motive in life is to be a "good fellow."

These comments should not be construed as an underestimation of the usefulness of the simple intellectual test as a preliminary precaution in engaging employees or in detecting extreme departures from the mode or average. The use of such tests in discovering such departures and variants as idiocy, imbecility and general stupidity has been amply justified by experience with them. But we are primarily concerned here with the determination of individual differences and qualifications within the large middle range of the curve of distribution. My conviction is that, in the case of the average individual, we must either:

1. Demonstrate that these important non-rational determinants of vocational aptitude and satisfaction correlate very, very closely with more strictly intellectual capacity;

2. Postpone the entire work of vocational guidance in these cases, on the basis of psychological examination, until that distant day when these characteristics can be approached by means of scales and norms; or

3. Otherwise guidance must rest, as it now largely does in democratic communities, on the broad knowledge of opportunity afforded by industrial and pre-vocational training, the encouragement of thorough and systematic self-scrutiny, and the method of repeated trials.

The first of these alternatives has scarcely been attempted; the second will probably not occur in our immediate generation; the third we have had always with us.

It is important to note that the employments here referred to are not "blind alley" occupations. They all offer possibilities of promotion and advancement which in the main are so open to competition that the individual inevitably tends to reach that level of responsibility, independence, opportunity and remuneration which his total equipment merits. It is also important that promotion or advancement by no means implies the continued use of the particular traits which distinguished the individual from his fellows on the lower levels of achievement. Thus the boy who enters business as a responsible clerk may often move on through the work of sales management, buying, general promotion, superintendency, and ultimate partnership. The capable artisan or mechanic may proceed from the work of general helper to that of special expert workman, foreman, superintendent, inspector, contractor, and commissioner of public works or postmaster general. Marked boyhood propensities for wood-work indicate neither that the lad is capable of moving through these very diverse steps of promotion, nor, on the other hand, that he must forever remain a journeyman or an expert workman.

Progress in these vocations does not then imply, in fact almost never does imply, merely increasing the quantity or quality of the work at which one starts. The promotion of a teacher is often from teaching and disciplining classes satisfactorily, to clerical assistance in the principal's office, the principalship, general school superintendence, administrative counselling and public lecturing, or the college or national presidency. The case of the teacher of biology who becomes the principal of a commercial high school is not at all unprecedented. For occupations of this character and for this main group of average individuals it is indeed hopeless to seek for vocational psychographs. It is here if anywhere that the general principle holds that one who does anything well could have done almost anything else well if he had cared to try. But the degree to which one *cares* is not measured by reaction time or cancellation tests. The question of the degree to which ability of one sort implies ability of other sorts is one of the several matters to be considered in a later chapter.

This fivefold division of the vocations is based on the degree to which the tasks involved require complete and normal psychological equipment. The foregoing consideration of these five main occupational groups may be said to constitute a brief summary of the present outstanding results of vocational psychology. The mentally incompetent can easily be discovered at an early age by the use of the graded intelligence scales. Their subsequent direction into forms of useful work appropriate to their degree of defect is not a psychological enterprise, but, rather, a civic obligation and industrial economy. The apparently small group of individuals who are by original nature fitted for the pursuit of work involving special or unit characters will, whether otherwise incompetent or generally capable, commonly demonstrate their unique abilities without the application of psychological technique. The much larger group of unspecialized workers, requiring rather higher degrees of mental competence, may be chosen without difficulty with the aid of the standard mental scales and norms, their academic records, and the judgments of their associates. These may be guided into such tasks as involve mainly a moderate degree of intellectual capacity and make no notable demand for the exercise of the social and moral virtues. The vocational psychology of the future will find its chief problems in dealing with the numerous and permanent tasks requiring workers who, in addition to their varying degrees of strictly intellectual proficiency, possess particular or complete instinctive, emotional and volitional equipment, and who are amenable to those social and educational agencies which seek to impress upon them the moral virtues of their community and age.

CHAPTER X

THE VOCATIONAL APTITUDES OF WOMEN

By

LETA STETTER HOLLINGWORTH, PH. D.

Bellevue Hospital, New York City

It is customary for authors, in discussing vocational problems, to assume that the vocational future of girls is determined in advance by the fact of sex. Not infrequently the lack of provision for domestic training in our high schools and colleges is indicated at length, and suggestions for establishing the domestic arts and sciences on a firmer basis in the educational system are advanced. Some paragraphs may be devoted to a discussion of the statistics which show that thousands of girls go from school into industry, and to an inquiry as to what training is best fitted to assist them in earning a living for the period intervening between graduation and matrimony. With this the discussion of vocational problems ends, so far as girls are concerned, and the remaining space is given over to more adequate consideration of the vocational aptitudes and guidance of boys.

It is the purpose of this chapter to inquire whether there are any innate and essential sex differences in tastes and abilities, which would afford a scientific basis for the apparently arbitrary and traditional assumption that the vocational future of all girls must naturally fall in the domestic sphere, and consequently presents no problem, while the future of boys is entirely problematical, and may lie in any one of a score of different callings, according to personal fitness. We shall try to determine whether the present expectation that all women will follow the same vocation, i. e., housekeeping, is founded on any fact or facts of human intellect, or whether it arises merely from ideas of traditional expediency connected with the care of the young, and whether it leads to a waste of energy and of intellectual talents.

The discussion will take the form of five general questions, together with the answers which are to be made to each in the light of experimental psychology: (1) Are there innate sex differences in average intelligence? (2) Is either sex more variable than the other in mental traits? (3) Are there any special causes of intellectual inefficiency affecting one sex but not the other? (4) Are there any sex differences in affective or instinctive equipment which would naturally lead to vocational differentiation of the sexes? (5) What explanation is to be given of the traditional division of labor between the sexes?

It will be necessary at the outset to draw a clear distinction between the *literature of opinion* and the *literature of fact*. The literature of opinion includes all written statements, made by scientific men and others, not based on experimental evidence. The literature of opinion on the subject of sex differences in mental traits is voluminous. It appears in the writings of Nietzsche, Schopenhauer, Mill, Möbius, and others. By the literature of fact is meant those written statements based on experimental data, which have been obtained under carefully controlled conditions, and which may be verified by anyone competent to understand and criticize them. In this chapter we shall seek the answers to the propounded questions in the literature of fact alone, neglecting as irrelevant to the discussion the entire literature of opinion.

Since the discussion is limited to the literature of fact, it will of necessity refer only to literature of a comparatively recent date. Until about fifteen years ago there had been practically no attempt to collect precise data on the subject of sex differences in mental abilities. Before experimental data were sought the hypothesis was accepted that human females are, by original nature, different from and inferior to human males, intellectually. The factor of sex determined everything; the way to discover whether a given individual was capable of any given intellectual task was not to let the individual undertake the task and to judge by the result, but to indicate the sex of the person in question.

Coincident with the intense controversy which rose in the nineteenth century over the higher education of women, a number of statistical studies were carried on by the questionnaire method. These were followed by experimental studies, and at the opening of the twentieth century several experiments were being made to investigate the matter of sex differences in intellect. About this time also the idea began to gain headway that whatever differences exist between the sexes as we find them in the world may be due to training and not to original nature; and it began to be pointed out that this aspect of the matter complicates even experimental investigation in ways difficult to control.

We may speak here of the experiments on brain weight which were published and much discussed about thirty years ago. Romanes, among others, insisted that the male brain was, on the average, several grams heavier than the female brain, and for a time it was supposed that the fact of innate female inferiority had been thus satisfactorily established. However, it was later demonstrated that relative to total body weight the female brain is as heavy as the male brain. It was also found that no positive correlation can be established between brain weight and intellect.

In 1906 Helen Bradford Thompson published her dissertation, from Chicago University, entitled "The Mental Traits of Sex." This volume gives a summary of the scattered bits of experimental work done previous to that time, and presents her numerous experiments on a group of men and a group of women at Chicago University. The result of her tests in various mental traits is that the differences between the sexes were in no case as great as the individual differences within either sex. Men differed from each other in these experiments (as did women also, among themselves), as much as men differed from women. In only two of the many traits tested was a reliable difference found between the central tendencies of the sexes. In speed of voluntary movement (tapping) men were quicker than women, and in memory women were superior to men. On the whole, however, the result indicated equality of mental ability between the sexes.[15] It will be enough for the present purposes to say that after about twenty years of collecting data by scientific experiment, the hypothesis that there is any innate sex difference in average intellectual ability has been abandoned by all psychologists who base their statements on scientific evidence. For example, Dr. E. L. Thorndike, in the most recent edition of "Educational Psychology" (1914), writes as follows, in summing up the experimental work on sex differences in average intellectual ability:

"The most important characteristic of these differences is their small amount. The individual differences within either sex so enormously outweigh any difference between the sexes that for all practical purposes any such difference may be disregarded.... As is well known the experiments of the past generation in educating women have shown their equal competence in school work of elementary, secondary and collegiate grade.... The psychologist's measurements lead to the conclusion that this equality of achievement comes from an equality of natural gifts, not from an overstraining of the lesser talents of women."

Thus our first question, Are there innate sex differences in average intelligence, which would call for differentiation of vocations on the ground of sex? may be thus answered: So far as the literature of fact tells us, we know of no considerable sex differences in average mental ability. The evidence of experimental science (and on this point there is now a large amount of evidence available) shows that by the test of averages the sexes have equal ability to perform mental tasks.

Our second question, Is there a sex difference in variability in mental traits which would call for a differentiation of vocation on the ground of sex? has not been so long, nor so thoroughly investigated by experimentalists as has the first question. What we are trying to discover here is whether, when tested in any given mental trait, a group of boys will differ more from one another than will a group of girls (similarly selected and equal in number) differ from one another. In other words, are the members of one sex very much alike in tastes, interests and abilities, while the members of the other sex differ over a wide range of tastes, interests and abilities? Obviously this might be the case, though the two groups yielded an average exactly the same in such traits. The answer to this second question will be of decided significance for vocational guidance. For example, if it were shown by experimental data that human females are, by original nature, rather closely alike, whereas human males differ from one another by wide extremes, we should have scientific grounds for concluding that social justice and social economy are well served by the present policy of guiding all females into a single occupation, while males are encouraged to enter the greatest possible variety of callings.

The first discussion of the comparative variability of the sexes was broached about a century ago by an anatomist, Meckel. It is very interesting (as well as amusing), in view of subsequent ideas about variability, to note what Meckel said. He thought the human female to be more variable than the human male, and he opined that, "since woman is the inferior animal and variability is a sign of inferiority," the conclusion was justified! Fifty years later, when Darwin put a different face upon variability, showing it to be an advantage and a characteristic affording the greatest hope for progress, the greater variability of the male began to be affirmed everywhere in the literature of opinion. Karl Pearson alone took issue with this view, which was current in the nineteenth century and is still widely credited, and pointed out that there existed as yet no literature of fact regarding comparative variability (though men of science had not on this account restrained themselves from uttering the most positive statements concerning it). Pearson thereupon actually gathered and computed hundreds of measurements of human beings, and presented his results in 1897, in a comprehensive article entitled "Variation in Man and Woman." He clearly demonstrated that there is, in fact, no indication of greater male variability, when actual anatomical measurements of adult human beings are treated with mathematical insight. Immediately Havelock Ellis, whose opinions were chiefly affected by Pearson's article, replied that when adults are made the subject of investigation, no information is gained regarding the matter of inherent or original differences in variability. Since birth, life and death, on account of social customs, etc., affect the sexes unequally, no one can say, in the case of adults, how much may be due to environment and how much to original nature. If Ellis had thought of this criticism before he wrote his own book, "Man and Woman," his chapter on "The Variational Tendency of Men" would certainly not have been published. However, his criticism of Pearson's material is no less just because he failed to apply it in his own case. It is true that measurements of adults do not tell us what might be the case with infants, who have not yet been subjected to the formative and selective influences of environment and training. Yet Pearson's article remained practically the only literature of fact regarding the comparative anatomical variability of the sexes until the year 1914. In 1914 Montague and Hollingworth published in the *American Journal of Sociology* an article setting forth in full the measurements of two thousand new-born infants, one thousand of each sex. The statistical result shows no difference whatever in variability between the sexes.

It may seem irrelevant to dwell upon anatomical data, when the purpose of this chapter is to deal with mental aptitudes. The pertinence of the data cited, however, lies in the fact that if any sex difference in physical variability could be established, this would suggest (though it would not prove) the existence of a sex difference in mental variability also. No experimental studies have ever been made for the express purpose of determining whether there exist sex differences in mental variability. Such scattered data as we possess have come incidentally from studies made with some other chief purpose in view. Such data were collected and summarized in the *American Journal of Sociology* for January, 1914. There was at that time very little evidence that could be cited on this subject, but such as there was gave no ground for maintaining the existence of any sex difference in variability. Since 1914 Trabue's experiments, with "completion tests," performed on about 1,300 school children, have been published; the Courtis arithmetic tests on several thousands of school children in New York have been made public; Terman has tested 1,000 unselected children by the Binet-Simon tests; and Pyle has undertaken his study in the measurement of school children. The evidence from these extensive experiments is in all cases that there is no sex difference in mental variability, as thus measured.

It is necessary also for the reader to bear in mind that there is as yet much controversy among those best equipped to understand the problems of variation, as to the proper methods of measuring comparative variability. The mathematical considerations involved need not be rehearsed here. But until it has been definitely determined just how comparative variability can be scientifically measured, it would seem premature to make any final statement as to sex differences in this respect.

We can therefore answer our second question thus: There is little or no agreement among those best qualified to speak, as to what constitutes the scientific method of measuring comparative variability. But according to the methods now deemed the most reliable, and according to those studies wherein presumably correct methods of measurement have been employed, there is no reason to suppose that there is any sex difference in variability, so far as the numerous traits tested are concerned. There has never been an experimental study made in which the sampling from both sexes was large, random, equal, and from groups of equal homogeneity socially and racially, that showed any reliable sex difference in variability. If we adhere to the literature of fact, we must conclude that, so far as we know, human females differ from each other as much as do human males in abilities and aptitudes.

We now come to the inquiry as to whether there are any special causes of intellectual inefficiency which affect one sex but not the other. Under this topic we may consider the periodic function, which characterizes girls and women, but which does not characterize boys and men. This periodic function has always been the object of superstition and taboo, and is such even among the civilized peoples of today. The literature of opinion is replete with references to it as a source of intellectual weakness and irresponsibility. We may let Frederick Harrison speak for a large group of writers on this point:

"Supposing all other forces equal, it is just the percentage of periodical unfitness which makes the whole difference between the working capacity of the sexes. It is owing to a very natural shrinking from hard facts, and a somewhat misplaced conventionality that this fundamental point has been kept out of sight."

The literature of opinion abounds in different notions, inconsistencies, and contradictory instances in the matter of the periodic function, and its alleged enormous influence on the intellectual and vocational life of women. Much of the opposition to the education of women was based on it, and it has even been exploited as a good reason why political freedom should be denied to women. It is positively stated that women are on this account unfitted to pursue professional and commercial life; yet it is not proposed that cooks, scrub women, mothers, nursemaids, housekeepers or dancers should be periodically relieved from their labors and responsibilities.

There is almost no literature of fact concerning the periodic function as related to the mental abilities of women. No effort had ever been made to subject this matter to study by instruments and methods of precision until very recently. Psychologists, while often stating the influence of periodicity on mental life to be fundamental and characteristic, entirely neglected to consider it when performing experiments on women subjects. In 1909 Voitsecovsky, at Petrograd, performed an experiment on six women by means of instruments of precision. He thought he found a positive result and that there was shown to be an actual influence of periodicity on certain mental functions. His conclusions are, however, largely invalidated by the fact that all his subjects knew the purpose of the experiment, and by the fact that he neglected to use, as a control, human beings not subject to the phenomenon in question. He also neglected to present his data in full, so that the reliability of his conclusions might be calculated.

Two studies of this phenomenon appeared in 1914. The first was a study by Dr. A. E. Arnold, as to the effect of school work on the periodic function, and this is reported in the January number of the *American Physical Education Review*. This investigator suspected, from his experience as a physician and teacher, "that much of the incapacity claimed was fictitious," and he determined, as an experiment, to institute a régime whereby no student under his supervision would be excused periodically from mental or physical duties, except in cases where some pathological condition existed. In summing up the data he says: "So far our results show all improvement [in the health of students]."

The second study, which appeared in 1914, was by the present writer. She made a prolonged and careful experimental study of twenty-three women (using as a control the records of men subjects), and failed to demonstrate any influence of periodicity on those mental abilities which she tested. These included speed and accuracy of perception, controlled association, steadiness, speed of voluntary movement, fatigability, and rate of learning.

A great amount of scientific work remains to be done before any final answer of any kind can be given to the question, Does functional periodicity exercise a fundamental and characteristic influence on the intellectual abilities of women? We must answer our third question in this way: There is very little experimental evidence on which to base a reply, but the few data which we do possess show no influence, either detrimental or beneficial.

Our fourth inquiry is this: Are there any innate sex differences in affective or instinctive equipment that would naturally lead to a vocational differentiation of the sexes? Here we must acknowledge ourselves to be entirely without a literature of fact. The literature of opinion is very extensive on the subject, and it would be an interesting and no doubt an instructive task to collect and summarize the various and conflicting opinions of men as to the affective and instinctive differences between the sexes. Men and women as we see them in the world do differ in affective behavior, but no one can say whether these differences in behavior are original or acquired. There are different conventional standards of emotional behavior for men and for women, but no one would be justified in saying that such standards arose from inherent affective differences between the sexes. The very variety that characterizes the statements on this subject constitutes proof of the ignorance of mankind in regard to it.

Since exact data are entirely lacking, the discussion of this last question need not detain us. We may, however, glance at one instinct which has repeatedly been stated to characterize women, and to constitute in itself a natural justification for differentiating the sexes vocationally. This is the "maternal instinct." Since the period of helpless infancy is very prolonged in the human animal, and since the care of infants is an exacting and onerous labor, it would be natural for those who are not biologically attached to infants, to use all means at their disposal to fasten the whole burden of infant-tending upon those who are originally so attached. We should expect this to happen, and it does happen. There has been a continuous social effort to establish as a norm the woman whose vocational proclivities are completely and "naturally" satisfied by child-bearing and child-rearing.

In the absence of all data, it would seem most reasonable to suppose that if it were possible to obtain a quantitative measurement of "maternal instinct," we should find this trait distributed among women just as we have found all other traits distributed, which have yielded to quantitative measurement. It is most reasonable to assume that we should obtain a curve of distribution, varying from an extreme where individuals have a zero or negative interest in the care of infants, through a mode where there is a moderate amount of impulse to tend infants, to a second extreme where the only vocational interest lies in such activity. The bearing and rearing of children is in many respects analogous to the work of soldiers. It is necessary to national existence, it means great sacrifice of personal advantage, and it involves suffering and danger, and, in a certain percentage of cases, the actual loss of life. Thus, as in the case of soldiers, every effort is and must be made to establish as a norm the extreme end of the distribution curve, where there is an all-consuming interest in patriotism, in the one case, and in motherhood in the other. In the absence of all scientific data, we should, therefore, guard against accepting as an established fact about human nature a doctrine that we might expect to find in use as a means of social control. It is also fitting to raise the question as to just what is meant by the term, "maternal instinct." Does it mean desire for offspring which are as yet non-existent? Does it mean only the tendency to care for helpless offspring after they are actually in existence? Does it mean an interest in children as such, regardless of their origin? Or does it consist in a mingling of all these elements? Above all, does it involve, as an essential element, an interest in waiting personally upon infants? One certainly gains the impression from a perusal of the extensive literature of opinion that to most persons the term is quite unanalyzed, and that it calls for analysis.

We have now considered four of our inquiries in the light of experimental evidence. We have discovered that a great amount of work remains to be done before we can answer most of them conclusively, and that to one question, at least, no answer at all can be given from the literature of fact. We can only say that, so far, scientific experiment has revealed no sex differences in the original nature of intellect that would imply a necessary differentiation of vocations on the ground of sex. There exist no scientific data to show (1) differences in average intellect; (2) differences in mental variability; (3) special causes of intellectual inefficiency affecting one sex but not the other; (4) differences in affective or instinctive equipment, implying a "natural" division of labor.

The division of labor between the sexes, which has existed through historic times and still persists, originated, so far as we know, in physiological, not in psychological differences. The momentous physiological fact that women bear and nourish infants and men do not, is the great primary sex difference on which our economic and vocational organization has been built up. It might be supposed that natural selection would have evolved an intellectual (or unintellectual) type in women, which could find its complete natural satisfaction in the vocation of child-bearing and child-rearing. But such a selection could take place only if mental traits were sex-limited in inheritance, or existed as secondary sex characteristics. No mental trait has ever been proved to be sex-limited in inheritance, or to exist as a secondary sex character. So far as we know, daughters inherit mental traits from fathers as well as from mothers, and sons inherit them from mothers as well as from fathers. Under such circumstances the law of natural selection can never become operative to solve the vocational problems of women.

The fact that women have not in the past equaled men in "philosophy, science, art, invention and management" is frequently adduced as evidence of their innate unfitness for pursuits other than the domestic. From such evidence, however, we glean in reality no information whatever about the vocational aptitudes of women. We should not expect any notable achievement by women in the fields mentioned above, for the following reasons. Women must bear and nourish infants, and men cannot. The period of gestation and the period of infancy are very protracted in the human species, together covering, for each infant reared, about six years. Until very recently no scientific methods of controlling procreation have been generally known or utilized. Thus women have borne great numbers of infants, all their youth and maturity being consumed by bearing and rearing young. The small minority of women whose lives happened not to be so consumed would be very unlikely to make any contributions in extra-domestic vocational achievement for two reasons. In the first place, all women were expected to mate and thus to procreate and rear offspring, and no provision was made by society for their training in lines other than those they would be expected to use. In the second place, those women who did not meet the common fate failed to do so for some special reason, such as ill health, mental disease, or the necessity of caring for decrepit relatives. The very causes of their celibacy would operate also against any vocational achievement on their part.

In the irrational trial and error method by which our human institutions have been developed, the logical expectation would be that the great physiological sex difference in reproductive function would probably influence vocational activities just as it has done. We find in the traditional division of labor between the sexes exactly what we should expect to find, even though there were an identity of intellectual abilities and interests. It seems both psychologically and socially desirable that the one incontestable conditioning factor in the vocational differentiation of men and women be raised clearly to consciousness, rather than submerged, as in the past, by an elaborate system of defense mechanisms and traditional devices of social control. It would be going afield from the immediate purpose of this chapter to offer constructive suggestions for such changes in economic and domestic management as might be necessary to overcome this conditioning factor, and thus to give free vocational opportunity to both sexes alike. To effect these changes in such a way that the maximum social betterment may be achieved thereby will be a task not simple but complex. It will call for the best thought and the most enlightened effort of which we are capable, and will be accomplished only with the passing of years and decades.

The essential thing at present is to know whether any basis for future action may now be found in the established facts of human nature. In the present state of scientific knowledge it would be as dogmatic (and therefore as undesirable) to state that significant sex differences in intellect do not exist, as to state that such differences do exist. All we can say is that up to the present time experimental psychology has disclosed no sex differences in mental traits which would imply a division of labor on psychological grounds. The social gain would be very great if the public could be brought to recognize intelligently that to many of the questions regarding the vocational aptitudes of women no definite answers can at present be given, because the necessary data for the formulation of answers have never been collected. So far as is at present known, women are as competent intellectually as men are, to undertake any and all human vocations.

FOOTNOTES:

[15] There was published in the October (1914) issue of the *Psychological Bulletin* a summary of all important experimental work done on sex differences in recent years. Any reader wishing to take up the evidence greatly in detail will do well to consult all of the references there given.

CHAPTER XI

THEORY AND PRINCIPLE OF PSYCHOLOGICAL TESTS AS APPLIED TO VOCATIONAL ANALYSIS

The more general questions of the theory of tests, their selection, evaluation, and technique of application and record, need not be considered here. The reader unfamiliar with these matters will find them fully treated in the various standard manuals of tests, and in numerous special articles and monographs referred to in the bibliography.

There are, however, certain particular aspects of the theory and use of mental tests which have special importance for vocational psychology. These are:

1. The question of the degree to which proficiency in one respect or ability or test implies proficiency in others.

2. The degree to which these intercorrelations are revealed by preliminary trials and modified by continued practice.

3. The question of the significance of preliminary trials in revealing the relative abilities of individuals as these would be shown after all the individuals had acquired their maximum skill or practice level of proficiency; that is, the relation between momentary capacity and ultimate achievement.

Attempts to intercorrelate mental or motor abilities as measured by laboratory tests have usually produced more or less irregular results. Some of the coefficients have been positive, some negative, but in only a few cases have many of them been large when the individuals tested have been chosen at random or with no deliberate intention of measuring only the extremes of the curve of distribution. Thus in a recent report of the correlations of abilities among several hundred adult individuals it is remarked that a certain test for logical memory is "one of the very best tests," partly because of "its high correlation with other tests" (an average correlation of .29).

Two reasons are largely responsible for these low coefficients. The first is the fact that the measures correlated have usually been initial trials, or at most averages of a very few trials. This means great individual variability and considerable consequent unreliability of the data. A more important factor, perhaps, is the fact that these preliminary trials do not necessarily represent the final capacities of the individuals. They are determined by a host of incidental or accidental influences and reveal only momentary ability, not ultimate capacity. There is every reason for expecting to find positive correlation of "desirable" traits, and we may well expect to find this increasingly true the more our measures test the final limits of capacity in the various tests. In other words, the only real correction for unreliable measures is to be made by continuing the test until the individual has reached the limit of practice in it.

Only occasional attempts have been made to determine the influence of practice on the correlation of abilities, and those that have been reported have been based on so few practice trials that no review of them need be given. In the present chapter I shall present the results of an experiment in which a group of observers were repeatedly tested until in each test a practice limit was approximated, a limit which, in most cases, one hundred further trials failed to improve. The results have a real interest for vocational psychology.

The experiment consisted in putting each of thirteen individuals through 205 repetitions of seven different mental tests. The trials were controlled as thoroughly as possible with respect to such factors as *interim* occupation, exercise, food, rotation of tests, temperature, illumination, and incentive and interest. The subjects, four women and nine men, ranging from eighteen to thirty-nine years in age, were mature, zealous, and faithful. Competition was stimulated by the award of desirable prizes, and each worker received a daily wage. Records were announced to the subjects only after each thirty-five trials. So far as previous practice in these particular tests is concerned, all the subjects were naïve. Five trials were made daily, these trials being distributed through the day at about two-hour intervals. The tests themselves occupied about forty minutes at each sitting.

The tests used were the following familiar laboratory forms:

1. Adding. Adding seventeen mentally to each of fifty two-place numbers and reciting aloud the correct answer. Order of numbers random at each trial. Record with stop watch, time required for perfect score.

2. Naming Opposites. Correctly naming opposites of each of fifty adjectives which occurred each time in random order. Record, time required for a perfect score.

3. Color Naming. The Columbia laboratory form of this test, with ten repetitions of each of twelve colors. Position of card changed at each trial. Record, time required for perfect score.

4. Discrimination Reaction. Discriminating between red and blue, and reacting correctly with appropriate hand. Record, average time, in *sigma*, and number of false reactions.

5. Cancellation. Crossing out digits from the Woodworth-Wells form of this test. Record, time required for 75 correct cancellations of equally difficult digits.

6. Coördination. The familiar three-hole test, for accuracy of aim. Record, time required for one hundred correct strokes.

7. Tapping. Executing four hundred taps at maximal speed, with hand stylus, right hand, elbow support. Record, time required.

Each test has been correlated[16] with all the remaining tests at various points in the curve of practice. Correlations were made at each of the following points:

1. Preliminary trial   designated 1st trial
2. Median of first 5 trials   designated 5th trial
3. Median of trials 20 to 25   designated 25th trial
4. Median of trials 75 to 80   designated 80th trial
5. Median of trials 200 to 205 designated 205th trial

At each of these points the thirteen individuals were arranged in an order of relative ability for each of the tests, and these orders were correlated with each other. Table 23 gives, for each test, at each point, the average correlation with all the other tests, and also the grand average correlations of all tests.

TABLE 23

SHOWING THE AVERAGE CORRELATION OF EACH TEST WITH ALL OTHERS, AT VARIOUS POINTS IN THE CURVE OF PRACTICE

Trial	Adding	Opposites	Color Naming	Discrimination	Coördination	Tapping	Final Average
1	.19	.10	.15	-.07	-.15	.17	.065
5	.41	.26	.15	.35	.21	.32	.280

25	.50	.35	.43	.27	.03	.35	.320
80	.55	.43	.53	.31	.18	.34	.390
205	.48	.62	.61	.35	.34	.52	.490

Except in the case of discrimination the effect of practice is to increase to a marked degree the intercorrelations of the various tests. Adding increases steadily up to the eightieth trial. Opposites and color naming gain even more steadily to the very end of the experiment, the increase in the coefficients being four to six fold. Tapping increases more slowly but no less certainly. In coördination the increase is very irregular, but the coefficients show, on the whole, a change from -.15 at the first trial to .34 at the finish. Only in the case of discrimination is there failure to increase after the fifth trial. In no case, after the preliminary trial, is there a negative coefficient among the average correlations, and indeed in only one case is there a coefficient smaller than .15. The final averages show steady increase from .065 at the preliminary to .28 at the fifth, .32 at the twenty-fifth, .39 at the eightieth, and .49 at the two-hundred-and-fifth trials. *With practice, then, the average correlations of all tests become positive, and the coefficients become greater the longer the practice is continued.*

In producing this increase in the intercorrelation of specific abilities through the medium of practice, at least three different factors probably coöperate. These factors have not an equal significance for vocational psychology and its interests in tests.

One of the least important of these factors is the variability of individual performance. In the beginning of the experiment each individual is more variable than at later points in the curve. This momentary variability need not be supposed to affect all the tests in the same way nor all individuals in the same direction. This fact may then tend somewhat to reduce the correlation of the preliminary trials and may in some cases materially affect the first five or ten trials. Beyond the twenty-fifth trial the variability in these tests is much reduced, and particularly so in the measures here used, which are in all cases, after the preliminary trial, the medians of five successive trials.

Another factor that deserves mention is the possibility of change in the character of the tests themselves, through practice with them. It is quite probable, for example, that the opposites test comes, after many repetitions, to resemble more and more that type of process or function involved in color-naming. The responses become more and more intimately associated with the stimulus words, the suggested responses to each word become more and more limited in number and in most cases reduced to a single word for each stimulus. This state of affairs is true of color-naming at the very beginning of the experiment. As the order of the stimulus words is changed at each trial, the test may come to involve more and more the simple task of giving merely the quickest possible association of the right response, and the overcoming of inhibitions and interferences of a more or less general sort, with less and less emphasis on the element of selection. Much the same may also be true of the addition test. It is in these three tests that the increase in correlation is most marked, and the actual coefficients highest at the end of the experiment. Careful analysis of what takes place as one improves in these simple tests would no doubt yield interesting material.

But these two factors—decrease in variability and change in the character of the tests—seem to be far from sufficient to account for the results. The tapping test remains much the same type of process throughout, the only apparent modifications consisting of slight changes in method and perhaps some gradual changes in the muscles. There is certainly no reason for suspecting that tapping and opposites or tapping and discrimination become, as tests, more alike because of frequent repetition. But the increase in correlation is clear in both these cases. Again, it is well established that the discrimination reaction, in the form here used, also tends to become reflex through practice, the conscious discrimination coming only after the correct reaction is made. These experiments called for between 3,075 and 4,100 single discrimination reactions on the part of each observer, which would afford ample time for such a change to show itself. Mere change in the character of the test would then lead us to expect color-naming, opposites, and adding to come more and more to resemble discrimination reaction. But they do not, if the coefficients may be taken as evidence. The coefficients of these tests with discrimination show no tendency to increase, even by the end of the experiment. The assumption of increasing similarity in the character of these pairs of tests would seem gratuitous. Moreover, if there were such increase in similarity, and this be also supposed to account for the higher correlation of color-naming and opposites with adding, coördination and adding should show the same increase in correlation. Just the reverse is actually the case, the correlation of coördination and adding decreasing consistently.

Some further factor must then be responsible for the general increase in correlation, aside from decrease in variability (which affects only the first few trials) and progressive qualitative approximation of the tests (which is seen to be inadequate). The doctrine of "general ability" or "general intelligence" at once suggests itself in this connection. If there is such a thing as "general ability" or "general intelligence," we should expect all samplings of that ability to correlate more and more as the measures came to be truer samples. We might indeed expect to find evidences of this general ability only when measuring the "ultimate capacity" of the individuals concerned. The momentary ability revealed in initial trials, or even in the first half-dozen trials, in a given set of tests might well be expected to show only low degrees of correlation. These trials would not be measures of ultimate capacity, but would be largely determined by previous practice, chance variability, momentary attitude and initial method of attack. They would, in short, be samplings only of momentary ability, not of final capacity.

Or if the assumption of a common factor be rejected, the present evidence tends strongly to support our earlier conclusion concerning the positive correlation between desirable mental functions. Some form of the doctrine of "general ability," at any rate, seems to be supported. But the conclusion seems to call for the qualification that "general ability" shall have reference to *final capacity* rather than to *momentary performance,* if the correlations are to be high. If each individual be given the opportunity to attain his limit of efficiency, his highest level of performance, then, when these final limits are reached, individuals who excel their fellows in one type of work will also tend to excel in other types of work.

The theory and practice of tests has in the past been too content to rest its claims on the meager results of a few preliminary samplings of an individual's ability. The fact that, even when a great variety of such samplings of a given individual are aggregated and balanced off against one another, few results of real diagnostic value are achieved should be sufficient warning against this tendency. My conviction is that for this purpose we shall find it necessary to determine the individual's "limit of practice" in the various tests before we shall secure diagnostic results which will be verified by the individual's subsequent achievement in daily life. We should know much more than we now know concerning the tendency and meaning of such correlations as show close relation between initial performance and ultimate capacity. This is particularly true if we wish to extend the method of tests beyond educational diagnosis and to use them as a means of vocational guidance or of industrial selection. For educational diagnosis we wish primarily to know what kind of practice the individual most needs. For vocational and industrial purposes we need rather to know what limits the individual can eventually reach, in given kinds of performance, as the result of practice, and to what degree his present equipment of incentive renders probable the actual achievement of this limit.

On the question of the significance of preliminary trials and the effects of practice on the relative standing of individuals in their group, there are important facts to be considered. In the direct application of mental tests it has too often been assumed that the actual performance of an individual, in one or a dozen trials at a given task, is in some way or other significant of that individual's final capacity in such work. It is true that several investigators have studied the effects of practice on individual differences. These workers were interested above all in questions as to relative rate of improvement, or amount or permanence of gain. Such studies have produced suggestive results, although they have been based, for the most part, on records of only a few subjects or on relatively few practice trials.

To what degree are individual differences after a given number of trials indicative of the final maximum capacity of the individuals concerned? At what various rates do the determining factors enter into the practice curves of a group of workers? What manner and amount of displacement in their relative order of ability are thus produced? At what point or points in the curves do the individuals assume their final order of relative capacity after training? How do the replies to these questions vary with the character of the task?

In the case of the experiments already described, record has been here taken of the following points in the curves of practice:

Preliminary trial   called initial trial

Median of trials 1 to 5   called 5th trial

Median of trials 20 to 25   called 25th trial

Median of trials 46 to 50   called 50th trial

Median of trials 76 to 80   called 80th trial

Median of trials 126 to 130 called 130th trial

Median of trials 171 to 175 called 175th trial

At each of these points the thirteen subjects were arranged in order of relative ability for the test at the given stage of practice. Each of these orders, or cross sections, of the group of practice curves was then correlated with the final order of position as shown in trials one hundred and seventy to one hundred and seventy-five. Table 24 gives the coefficients of correlation derived in this way. A careful study of this table will prove instructive.

TABLE 24

Showing the Correlation of Ultimate Capacity with Capacity at Different Points in the Curve of Learning

(See Text for Explanation)

The Test	Preliminary	5th Trial	25th Trial	50th Trial	80th Trial	130th Trial	Final Trial 175th
Adding	.15	.19	.87	.87	.97	.96	1.00
Opposites	-.08	.62	.49	.83	.94	.98	1.00
Color Naming	.68	.89	.86	.91	.97	.97	1.00
Discrimination	.68	.62	.60	.50	.50	.79	1.00
Cancellation	.67	.68	.88	.69	.93	(1.00)	—
Coördination	.52	.79	.77	.90	.95	(1.00)	—
Tapping	.23	.48	.63	.68	.69	.89	1.00
Averages	.41	.61	.73	.77	.85	.92	1.00

It is at once evident that the preliminary trial is by no means always a measure of the final relative capacities of the individuals tested. The average of all seven coefficients increases from .41 at the preliminary trial to .92 at the one hundred and thirtieth trial. As the trials proceed then, the relative positions of the thirteen individuals become more and more definitely fixed, but in the beginning the indication is obscure. The rate of this process, however, varies with the test, and to a considerable degree. Adding shows changes in position which effect a correlation of .87 only after the twenty-fifth trial. Beyond this point there is little change, the eightieth and one hundred and thirtieth trials correlating equally well, and practically perfectly, with the final order. After twenty-five trials, then, the final capacities of the individuals in the adding test may be said to be indicated fairly accurately. Opposites, in the fiftieth trial, yields a coefficient equal to that of addition in the twenty-fifth trial, and by the eightieth trial the correlation may be said to be complete. Only after fifty trials, then, can the test be said to yield comparative measures which reflect the individual's final capacity in this form of controlled association. In the case of tapping it is only at the one hundred and thirtieth trial that the correlation with final position exceeds .69.

These results may be easily comprehended by thinking of each test (as for instance the tapping test) as a prolonged race, consisting of a large number of heats (205 separate trials). All individuals begin with a running start, their respective initial speeds depending on the momentum they have acquired through a certain amount of previous practice, and on such momentary ability and zeal as they possess at the time. But as the succeeding "heats" or trials occur some individuals who were originally in the lead begin to lose ground in relation to others who, though initially slower, are now speeding up and overtaking the leaders. Still others may retain their original relative positions to the end of the race. In the table of coefficients, a correlation of 1.00 indicates that at that point the ultimate relative positions of the contestants have at last become established. The nearer the figure approaches zero the more uncertain are the relative positions at the particular trial. To terminate the race at a point where the correlation is low and to reward the contestants according to the position they had reached at that point would be manifestly unfair to those who were still speeding up and partial to those who were losing ground.

Color-naming, discrimination, cancellation, and coördination show up to much greater advantage. Even the preliminary trials in these tests show fairly high correlations with the final orders. The first two of these show little change as practice proceeds. In the case of the latter two tests, although the initial correlations are fairly high, there is nevertheless considerable increase as the trials proceed.

The meaning of these results seems to be that before one attempts to interpret individual differences as disclosed by performance in such a series of simple tests, he should have clearly in mind the distinction between temporary proficiency and ultimate capacity. If he is interested, for example, in determining the vocational prospects of a youth, or the relative merits of candidates or culprits, it is important that he realize that relative abilities in many of these laboratory tests may be changed quite beyond recognition by continued work. It is highly desirable to know more than we now know concerning the degree to which initial and intermediate trials in these tests reflect final capacity. In the past the question seems hardly to have been asked.

Individual differences in early trials, in some tests, are fairly significant of the working level to which the performer may be brought later. In other tests this is not the case. On the significance of these early trials may depend, in many cases, the vocational value of the particular test.

Changes in the nature of the tests, variations of methods of attack, and specific improvement in the directness, independence and rapidity of the special nervous connections concerned—these three factors would all declare themselves in the form of "changes in ability." A useful piece of work in the case of all tests will be the analysis of the nature of the changes resulting from practice. But in any case the presence of these changes in correlation shows that we are not, in early trials, measuring the same tendency or capacity in all performers. The concrete tasks of daily life doubtless show just such qualitative changes, during practice, as we may suppose to be present in some of these tests. Just as it is ultimate capacity in daily life that is, with a given set of incentives, most important, so in the laboratory the measurement of "ability after practice" ought to be more emphasized than it is at present.

If it is true that with practice all tests correlate with one another, so that an individual who is good in one type of work is also, when his practice level has been reached, good in other types of work, the task of vocational psychology is at once enormously simplified. In place of further search for special occupational tests adapted in some peculiar way to particular types of work, our task is rather that of extending the general intelligence scales until they represent higher and higher degrees of general ability.

It is quite probable that further advance in this direction will come, not from the elaboration or invention of more tests, but by the selection of a very few tests, and the examination of the final limits of practice with respect to them. The problem will then be the selection of sets of tests in which initial performance shows high correlation with ultimate capacity in the tests themselves, or else the laborious and undramatic, but perhaps preferable, alternative of continuing every test until the practice limit is reached by the individual. In the latter case it would be well to learn more about the nature and range of these limits than we know at present.

In so far as particular tasks are actually found to call for highly specialized aptitudes, for the detection of which tests are sought, there will be the further problem of correlating these various tests with the particular aptnesses or fitnesses toward the detection of which diagnosis is directed.

There will also be the problem of the alignment of the various types of work along the general intelligence scales, as rapidly as these are extended and elaborated. In so far as this method is followed, the task of selecting from candidates those best fitted for the accomplishment of special types of work will be easily handled. Vocational selection will readily find methods suited to its purposes. But vocational guidance, as distinguished from vocational selection, must for some time to come depend largely on the determination of interests, incentives, satisfactions, emotional values and preferences, and the discovery and direction of these through general channels of information and through the methods of industrial and pre-vocational education.

This is a hard and an arduous program. It calls for strenuous work on the part of investigators, patience and faithfulness on the part of observers, and wide coöperation of investigators with each other. From the immediately practical point of view it also offers an inviting opportunity to those foundations and individuals who are interested in supporting the further development of "the arts of social control over human nature."

FOOTNOTES:

[16] For explanation of the technique and meaning of correlation see the footnote on p. 45.

CHAPTER XII

CONCLUSION

The leading problems of vocational psychology we have seen to be three in number: First, how may the individual achieve the most adequate knowledge of his own peculiar mental and instinctive constitution, his equipment of capacities, tendencies, interests and aptitudes, and the ways in which he compares, in these respects, with his fellows? Second, how may the individual acquire information concerning the general or special traits required for successful participation in the various vocations, in order to select a line of activity for which he is constitutionally adapted? Third, how may the employer determine the relative desirability, fitness and promise of those who may offer themselves as his associates and assistants, or for minor positions in his employ? Obviously, if vocational psychology were in its maturity, rather than in its infancy, these various questions would resolve themselves into a single problem. The traits required in the various types of work would be fully known and specified, so that both the choice of the individual and the selection by the employer would proceed directly, once the individual's characteristics were known.

From this goal we are very far, but by no means hopelessly, removed. As we have seen in the preceding chapters, the line of attack is being advanced very unevenly at its various points. It is indeed characteristic of any new branch of science that it does not advance symmetrically and at a uniform rate, but moves ahead, now in this direction, now in that, so that the line of complete development is some distance behind the outposts of exploration. So in the case of vocational psychology we may draw a rough line which shall represent the main region of advance, and may indicate the various points where the line lags behind or goes conspicuously forward.

The main line of advance has left far behind it the magical ritual of primitive thought, the medieval search for significant omens and clairvoyant signs, the pseudo-scientific faith in the structural characteristics elaborated in physiognomy and phrenology, and has taken its stand firmly at the point where emphasis is laid on the objective study of the individual's behavior. Educationally this position shows itself in the abandonment of the purely disciplinary ideal of abstract training, and the substitution of training in specific forms of conduct, exercise, and occupation, accompanied by concrete experience with industrial opportunities, rewards, and satisfactions. From the more strictly psychological point of view the position shows itself in the experimental application of mental tests. In the measurement of the more strictly intellectual capacities, the line has shown a very decided advance since the beginning of the present century. The available intelligence scales make possible the diagnosis of intellectual defect, normality or precocity in units of considerable reliability, in the case of pre-adolescents. This step in itself is sufficient to put educational, industrial and social enterprise deeply in debt to the new science of experimental psychology.

But this by no means constitutes the only point of marked advance. Thanks to the elaboration of more complex and more diversified tests, and the gradual accumulation of norms, it is now possible to make mental measurements in the case of individuals considerably beyond the age of adolescence. By means of such methods, degrees of sensitivity, dexterity, accuracy, speed, comprehension, docility, discrimination, ingenuity, information, observation, and numerous other general aspects of mental alertness may be recognized. Comparison of such measures, in the case of adult workers with actual success in the field of their activity, tends constantly to show high degrees of positive correlation. The fact that the correlations are not perfect raises numerous problems, the solution of which is now being attempted.

The evidence now at hand suggests that the incomplete correlation comes, in part at least, from the fact that some of the tests of momentary achievement do not fully represent the ultimate capacities of the individuals measured. At this point the line is relatively slow in advancing. The obstacles encountered consist partly in our incomplete information concerning which of the tests at once reveal final capacity and which do not. This information must necessarily come slowly because of the difficulties involved in securing the coöperation of subjects who will submit to the prolonged series of measurements which such investigations involve. Such data as are available, while inadequate to constitute proof, suggest very strongly that those tests which are now in most common use correlate closely with each other when the limit of practice is reached in all of them. If subsequent work confirms this suggestion, the determination of the factor of general intelligence may proceed on either of two bases. Either we may use a very few trials of tests in which such trials may be found to indicate ultimate capacity, or we may use a small number of tests, but continue the measures until the limits of practice are reached.

But there is probably another factor in part responsible for the incompleteness of the correlations between test records and direct measures of vocational success. This is the fact that characteristics other than general intelligence play a conspicuous part in daily life. The interests, the incentives, the emotions, and the equipment of instinct and habit, which show themselves in such traits as curiosity, competition, honesty, loyalty, promptness, patience, the play impulse, etc., do not count for nothing in vocational activity. Moreover, it is quite likely that, in addition to the common fund of intelligence, each individual possesses in his or her own degree, certain more specialized capacities and aptitudes, for the complete measurement of which the available tests are inadequate. The graded "product scales," however, represent a definite step toward the measurement of many of these specific capacities.

Another difficulty encountered at this point is the fact that such direct measures of vocational success as have been utilized in these comparisons are in themselves subject to very large error. Only in recent years, and as a result of the emphasis of the human factor in industry, has it come to be the common practice to secure adequate records of the work of the individual as contrasted with the work of the gang. Even today such records are available in accurate form for only the simpler operations, in which standardized conditions of work can be maintained. The relative success of salesmen, for example, is not fairly measured in terms of the amounts of their sales, the number of prospects interviewed, or the frequency with which the assigned tasks are accomplished, unless the local trade conditions of the respective territories are fully taken into account. Inasmuch as such errors of measurement tend to reduce the apparent correlation between the traits measured, it is extremely probable that the psychological tests are even more significant than their present results indicate. Refinement of the tests must be accompanied by more accurate and precise measurement of the actual working efficiency of individuals in the industrial field, if the results of the one are ever to represent the amount of the other. In this as in many other respects, the development of vocational tests depends as much upon the active and intelligent coöperation of industrial concerns as it does upon the enthusiasm and diligence of the psychological investigators.

From the point of view of the employer, the incompleteness of the correlation between tests and direct measures is of little concern. Even a very small positive correlation affords him a degree of guidance in the selection of his workers that was far from forthcoming under the haphazard methods of employment that have been traditional. But from the point of view of the individual who is seeking guidance, or who is accepted or rejected on the basis of his performance in psychological tests, any correlation which is imperfect may lead to occasional injustice and misdirection.

The diagnosis of the instinctive and attitudinal characteristics and the recognition of the more specialized aptitudes constitute two points at which the line of advance is relatively slow. It is at these points that the psychographic methods find their task. As we have already seen in detail, the methods of the individual and the vocational psychograph are still in the stage of empirical procedure. In this stage of their development nearly any effort to amplify or apply them is certain to contribute results of positive value. The recent studies that have contributed most notably toward the further development of the psychographic technique have been in the form of the specialized vocational tests and methods. Such studies, in addition to yielding results of immediate applicability in the description and analysis of the special tasks at which they are directed, also constitute positive progress towards the more elaborate psychographic pictures of individuals and of tasks.

Meanwhile groups of further problems have been definitely organized, and preliminary steps taken toward their solution. The formulation of systematic guides to self-analysis and introspection and the study of the reliability to be placed in the individual's estimates of his own characteristics are making definite and interesting progress. The examination of the time-honored "recommendation" and the estimates of associates and friends, and the investigation of the accuracy of such judgments as are based on these testimonials, on letters of application, on the school records, etc., have already thrown long-desired illumination on several aspects of vocational psychology. The effort to base the vocational endeavors of women on the data of exact inquiry, rather than on the maintenance of primitive taboos and domestic and literary traditions, has played its own valuable part in one of the most vital economic adjustments of our age.

The very fact that a systematic presentation of the problems and methods of vocational psychology is possible signifies an enormous advance beyond the very recent stage in which all vocations were mysteries, all choices a serious form of gambling, and all employment confessedly a matter of impressionistic prejudice. To those who become familiar not only with the program of this new branch of applied science, but as well with the outstanding definite and positive contributions which that program has already yielded, the words of a constructive pioneer in this branch of scientific inquiry seem to be already becoming a statement of fact, rather than the mere expression of a hope. "The nineteenth century witnessed an extraordinary increase in our knowledge of the material world, and in our power to make it subservient to our ends; the twentieth century will probably witness a corresponding increase in our knowledge of human nature, and in our power to use it for our welfare."

CPSIA information can be obtained
at www.ICGtesting.com
Printed in the USA
BVHW021137210323
660854BV00010B/224